SPECIAL AGENT SCULLY

THE GILLIAN ANDERSON FILES

MALCOLM BUTT

Plexus, London

Copyright © 1997 by Malcolm Butt
Published by Plexus Publishing Limited
55a Clapham Common Southside
London SW4 9BX
First Printing 1997

British Library Cataloguing in Publication Data

Butt, Malcolm
    Special Agent Scully :
    the Gillian Anderson files
    1. Anderson, Gillian
    2. Television actors and actresses -
    United States - Biography
    I. Title
    791.4'5'028'092

ISBN 0 85965 254 8

Printed in Great Britain by
Hillman Printers, Frome
Cover designed by Phil Smee
Book designed by Phil Gambrill

ACKNOWLEDGEMENTS:

The following Internet sites proved
invaluable in researching this book:
http://www.ecr.mu.oz.au/~simc/xf/people/GA,
run by Simon Chin and
http://tempest.ucsd.edu:80/~jlinvill/xfiles/gillian
run by Mike Quigley.
    The following publications were
also extremely helpful: the *Radio Times*,
the *Philadelphia Enquirer*, *BC Woman*, *FHM*,
the *Sun*, the *Sunday Telegraph* (UK), the *Sunday
Telegraph* (Sydney), *SFX*, *Starlog*, the *Observer*,
New Woman, *Sci-Fi Buzz* magazine, *Movieline*
magazine, *News of the World Sunday* magazine,
TV Week, *Melbourne Herald Sun*, *US* magazine,
Okay weekly, the *Telegram Tribune* (California),
the *Los Angeles Times*, the *Washington Post*.
Also the following books were vital: *The X-Files
Confidential* by Ted Edwards (Little, Brown);
Deny All Knowledge: Reading The X-Files
by David Lavery, Angela Hague and
Marla Cartwright (Faber and Faber);
Anderson and Duchovny: An Extraordinary Story
by David Bassom (Hamlyn). Thanks also to Joe
Roach, The Harco Political Research Unit, Ian
Schirmer and Rise Media.

Grateful thanks to the following photographic
agencies for supplying photographs: All Action;
All Action/Jean Cummings; All Action/
FotoBlitz; All Action/Fox Broadcasting; All
Action/Photoreporters/Ian Gatchal; All
Action/Nader Group; All Action/Poya; All
Action/Photoreporters/Phil Roach; All
Action/Syd; All Action/Photoreporters/Joyce
Silverstein; All Action/Paul Smith; All
Action/Fox Broadcasting/Ken Staniforth; Alpha;
Alpha/S.Finn; Corbis/Everett; Corbis/Everett/
Fox Broadcasting; Corbis/Everett;
Corbis/Everett/Jack Rowand; Retna; Retna/
Armando Gallo; Retna/Steve Granitz;
Retna/Patsy Lynch; Retna/Bruce Malone;
Retna/Gregory Pace; Retna/John Spellman;
Retna/Robert Spencer; Scope Features; Scope
Features/DMI/Mirek Towski. Cover photograph
by All Action/Jean Cummings. Further thanks
also to the following publications: *The Box*; the
Daily Mirror; the *Daily Express*; *Esquire*; *Melody
Maker*; the *Rolling Stone*; *Sky Magazine*; *X Posé*.

JAPAN, 16 JUNE 1996

Garuda Flight 865 to Bali taxied across the tarmac, ready and on schedule for take-off from Japan's Fukoka airport. Once Flight Control had given the all-clear, the pilot accelerated the aircraft powerfully along the runway, but almost immediately he began experiencing problems, and emergency procedures were launched. Hurtling along at speed, the plane swerved out of control and slammed into the ground, scratching a massive gorge in the runway. The plane skidded along on its underside for some five hundred metres before grinding to a halt and bursting into flames, its fuselage gutted and minus its wings, tails, engines and wheels. Miraculously no one was killed, although three hundred passengers were injured, some seriously. For those in the accident it was a trauma that will scar them for the rest of their lives.

One lady, relaxing in a hotel and unaware of this disaster, was considerably more lucky: she had been scheduled to take Flight 865 but at the last minute had cancelled due to work commitments and booked on to the next flight. Oblivious to her close escape, she landed safely at Bali and proceeded through customs to be met by her work colleagues. As she pushed her trolley through the Arrivals door, she noticed with a wry smile a man from a travel agent called 'X', waiting for his new clients, whose name was scribbled on his clipboard – a family called Scully.

Chicago, 23 August 1974

Carl Kolchak smelt something strange. He had been called to a supposedly routine murder site. When he arrived he immediately felt unsettled. Apparently, the girl had died in a river of sand. There were no footprints and no blood. How come?

It looked like it would be another peculiar investigation for Kolchak, but he was used to this; indeed, this was what he loved. After all, he had faced far worse situations than this in his years of detective work. Take, for example, the werewolf, the Indian demon, the mummy, the aliens and of course the vampire . . .

At the moment the stake was driven through the vampire's heart, a teenage Chris Carter, sitting in his cosy hometown of Bellflower, southern California, could not have been more terrified. He loved *The Night Stalker* and thoroughly enjoyed being frightened out of his wits each week. *The Twilight Zone* was another favourite, but it was *The Night Stalker* that really scared him.

It scared a lot of other people too. Mid-seventies America was still reeling in the aftermath of the monumental exposure of Watergate and their President's subsequent resignation. Reinforced by the Pentagon Papers and undermined by the rosy images of an ultimately futile intervention in Vietnam, the basic belief that Uncle Sam was always honest was starting to be questioned seriously. Not by Chris Carter and his young friends, of course: they were just scared senseless. However, his elders cocked an ear at Kolchak's bizarre cases and even more odd-ball theories, half intrigued and half-worried.

Over ten years later and Carter, now editor of *Surfing* magazine, was constantly writing. About surfing, yes, but also about other, more weird stuff. His degree in journalism had taught him well, and through his job and his background he was drawing on a strange mixture of traditional education, a surfing lifestyle, childhood influences, and modern paraphernalia, all mixed together into reams and reams of fiction. After thirteen years at the surfing publication, he progressed to Disney and began writing some sit-coms, including *Cameo By Night*, *A Brand New Life* and *Rags To Riches*. In 1993, Carter's career took another upward turn when he was head-hunted by Fox Network to develop their programming schedule. He was delighted – he could finally put forward some of his more outlandish ideas, and he had one script particularly in mind.

Chris Carter's lengthy journalistic and media background included work for Surfing *magazine and Disney before he conjured up* The X-Files.

The show he took to Fox executives was to be called *The X-Files*, and rested on a simple premise. It would be based around a maverick FBI agent, Fox Mulder, whose fascination with all things paranormal brought him into contact with a host of absurd situations and people. The show would follow this agent, along with his colleague, Dana Scully, on their various weird encounters. Simple premise, brilliant idea: complicated show. Carter felt there was ample material for a weekly series, and he was convinced there was a market; he was acutely aware of the growing public interest in the supernatural, the extraterrestrial, and conspiracy theories. The same seed that had made Kolchak's *Night Stalker* such a success in the seventies had blossomed so much that it was no longer a joke to say you believed in aliens. Hundreds of books, magazines, and societies now existed which fuelled the fascination with this area, and Carter saw *The X-Files* as a natural progression from this.

Fortunately, the Fox executives tentatively agreed and a small budget was agreed to film a pilot episode – after that, as with all television shows, if the audience wasn't sufficient then the show would be dropped. Carter assembled a team around him, but based that first script very much on his own work. Auditioning for the new show went well and within a short space of time it was clear that the role of Fox Mulder was filled. A seasoned actor, David Duchovny, who had already appeared in several feature films and shows including *Working Girl*, *Julia Has Two Lovers* and, most poignantly, David Lynch's surreal *Twin Peaks*. With his deadpan delivery, cool looks and considerable experience, Duchovny seemed ideal for the part.

The role of his colleague Scully was, however, proving to be somewhat more difficult to cast. Fox Network wanted a busty blonde (nice legs would be a bonus), and plenty of television and film experience. There were several promising names on the list for the audition, although one, Gillian Anderson, seemed to be wholly unsuitable. According to her résumé, she had only one previous television show under her belt, and even that was merely a single appearance for a programme that flopped. Already uninterested, the executives enthused even less when she walked into the room. Standing at just over five feet tall, with a prominent Roman nose, she had just an average figure, which was hardly complimented by the dour, baggy suit she wore. The Fox executives were not remotely interested.

Chris Carter was. In his mind, he had just seen Special Agent Scully walk into the room.

THE ENDLESS MILL

For Gillian Anderson, this was yet another appointment in the endless mill of auditions she had been attending in Los Angeles, all of which were swamped by hundreds of aspiring actresses. In the past year alone she had attended over 150, and the only difference with this latest one for Fox was that it landed on the day after her last unemployment cheque had arrived. Without that regular financial boost, maybe her luck was at an end. She had come a long way and persevered to get this far; in fact, she had done well, but maybe it was time to move on.

She had been moving on all her life. By the age of eleven she had lived in three separate continents and in many different homes. Life started for Gillian Leigh Anderson in Cook County's St Mary's Hospital near the Windy City of Chicago, on 9 August 1968, born to proud parents Edward and Rosemary Anderson. Before she was out of nappies the Anderson family uprooted, and headed two thousand miles into the Caribbean sea to the hurricane-prone island of Puerto Rico, where her father's expertise in film post-production had landed him a job. This was a fairly temporary post and within a matter of months the Andersons had once again packed their bags, this time heading for London, where the two-year-old Gillian would spend the next nine years. It was 1970, and in Swinging London, the Beatles had just broken up.

Gillian was a playful child and loved nothing more than cutting up worms in the garden and planting their dismembered remnants as if they were flowers. The early days in the city were financially very tight for the family, but as they settled in things began to get easier – her father was studying at the London Film School in Covent Garden, and her mother was a computer analyst. After a brief period in Stamford Hill Gillian started school, aged five, attending Coleridge Junior School in Crouch End, north London.

As with any school, any slight deviation from the norm is a prime target for bullies, and Gillian's strange accent was immediately picked up on as perfect fodder for taunting. Gillian told *Okay Weekly* of these difficult times: 'I took a lot of stick – probably because I was American, even though I did speak with an English accent. But I was also very independent and bossy, which didn't exactly help. I wasn't a particularly bright student – I was too much of a daydreamer. And I certainly wasn't science-mad like Scully. I didn't pay attention, I talked a lot and got punished a lot.'

Gillian enjoyed a normal, albeit itinerant, childhood,
but began to 'go off the rails' at High School.

Although she was bullied and teased, Gillian soon learned to look after herself. After a while she cultivated her own circle of friends, and began to enjoy school and her new life in London. She even had a boyfriend when she was aged eight: Adam, who was the first 'man' she ever kissed. It was not a serious relationship, however (he didn't get much pocket money) and Gillian wasn't yet aware of the ways of the world that older boys at school talked about: 'I was very into swearing as a child. I remember asking my mom what fuck meant, what fucking was, and I can't remember on my life what her response was. I remember hearing it in the playground when I was eight, off a kid who was twelve. He fancied me and I fancied him but I was scared to death because his affection was like grown-up affection – he may have even done the fuck word. And I had no idea what it meant.'

By 1976 London's music scene was about to explode with the inflammatory arrival of the Sex Pistols. Punk rock, with its radical chic, noisy music and drug-abusing anti-stars, although reviled by the staid British establishment of the time succeeded in revolutionising not only music, but also fashion, art, the media, and modern culture in general. Gillian was only eight, but the unconventional atmosphere in the English capital inevitably rubbed off on her and she loved it. By the time she approached her eleventh birthday, she was very happy – her school friends were a close-knit group, she enjoyed her education and loved London. So it was with understandable indignation that she reacted when her father took another job, which would mean relocating again – this time to the small town of Grand Rapids in Michigan. The London film market was too depressed for Edward to find enough work, and they had no choice but to move (he would eventually start his own post-production company, called Gillian). Despite her protestations, Gillian was once more wrenched away from the place she had come to call home.

David Letterman: 'What was life like for you while you were growing up there?'
Gillian Anderson: 'It was, uh . . . it was different. It was normal and it was strange.'
David Letterman: 'Normal and strange? How so? How do you reconcile those things?'
Gillian Anderson: 'Grand Rapids, I guess, is pretty normal. I was strange.'

Once Gillian saw her new home town in Michigan she was even more opposed to the enforced move. Compared to London, Grand Rapids was like a ghost-town. The initial predicament of being an outsider in London, speaking with a strange accent, was now repeated in reverse. During her nine

Gillian as a child in England.

years in England she had inevitably picked up some idiosyncrasies of that culture and now considered herself to be British (the adult Gillian considers herself an American). Attending Fountain Elementary School, she was once again teased and bullied, which made her become withdrawn and subsequently christened the class 'weirdo'. A fiery and independent young girl, this added to her estrangement from her school peer group.

The overnight contrast in her lifestyle was dramatic. From the sophisticated whirlwind of metropolitan London to the sleepy prairie town (and frequently right-wing) environment of the Midwest, there was a gulf between the two that Gillian hated. She missed her friends in London, she missed the city, and she was unsettled at home. She was very unhappy, as her mother recalled in the *News of the World Sunday* magazine: 'Gillian was devastated. Her friends in North London were very hip city kids. The boys wore earrings and the girls were very fashionable. We were all sad. We loved London and hated the idea of moving back to the Midwest.'

Such a maelstrom of feelings is hardly a positive thing for any pubescent girl, and this soon proved to have a negative effect on Gillian's formative years. By the time she moved up to the City High School, her grades were poor and her attitude worse. The cultural void between Blighty and the USA caused great trouble for the teenage Gillian, as her mother continues: 'Her classmates all thought she talked funny because she didn't have an American accent. Gillian had to learn to speak like an American for the first time in her life, just to fit in. Another problem was spelling. American English has dozens of words that are spelt slightly differently from how they are in England, and she had to learn to make that adjustment.' It was not that she wasn't clever, she was just unsettled. Fortunately, after some time had elapsed, the young Gillian had readjusted to her new surroundings and her grades began to improve a little: 'She did extremely well in school considering the upheaval. The teachers said that she was two years more advanced than her classmates. She worked very hard to fit in.'

Despite these positive signs, when Gillian hit her mid-teens, she began to go off the rails. As is so often the case, the bullied became the bully and she adopted a much more aggressive manner. After a summer-holiday visit to their London flat (which the family had kept on after the move to Michigan) Gillian transformed herself. In London, punk was still the rage and she loved it, so on her return she had her nose pierced, shaved her plaits off and swapped her neat brown cords for size-seven combat boots and $2 dresses. In came the tapes of Lords of the New Church, Dead Kennedys and Velvet Underground, and out went the homework, study and good grades. Red hair and revealing mini-skirts were soon displaced by black and purple hair and more outlandish gear – at one point she sported a two-foot-high purple mohican. She also went through a phase of dressing herself all in black.

Still worse, aged thirteen she lost her virginity ('It was awkward, stupid, unadulterated crap') to a man much older than herself, a singer in a dodgy punk rock band, and a part-time bedsit poet. This man later evolved (if you can call it that) into a neo-Nazi, and unwittingly started one of the biggest media myths about Gillian Anderson – that she lost her virginity to a fascist, although he only became so politically inclined many years after his relationship with Gillian had ended. Even so, it is unlikely he was the most endearing of people at this time. The odd couple frequented dingy gigs and smashed themselves against the 'moshing pit' of fans, swearing at passers-by on the way home, or at anyone who stared at their unusual looks. Gillian's parents, her father in particular, were not pleased by these latest developments. Rather immaturely, she would walk along on his left side, so that he couldn't see the offending nose ring.

The following year Gillian went one better – she moved in with the older man. They would sleep rough in disused warehouses and friends' flats, and his stories of loser buddies shooting up in coffee-houses kept her intrigued for nearly three years. In such an environment, Gillian found herself slipping into

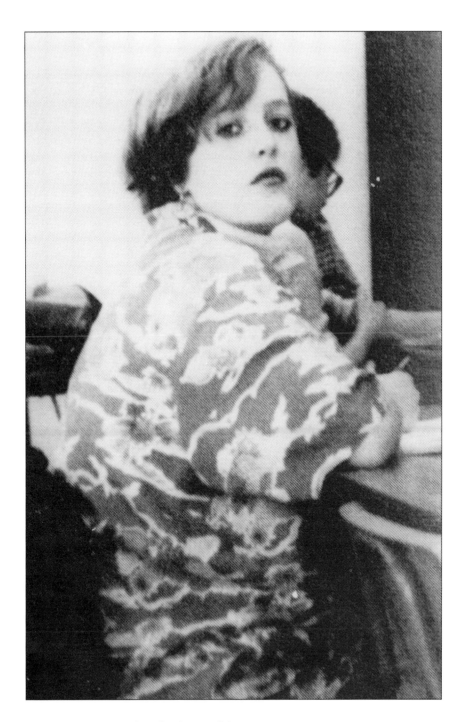

*Gillian was tired of school by the age of thirteen
and this was reflected by her poor grades.*

promiscuity and drinking, and would often buy her boyfriend food, beer and cigarettes. Years later a tabloid newspaper article hinted at alleged drink problems, and although stopping short of an admission, Gillian clearly remembers difficult times – she has talked of 'separation anxieties', of 'hurting myself in various ways', and has publicly identified with the anorexic teenage character, played by Jane Horrocks, in Mike Leigh's film *Life Is Sweet*. The promiscuity was a desperate façade that hid Gillian's insecurities, as she told *FHM* magazine: 'During college I was somewhat promiscuous. Not in a bad way. But it wasn't fun. I like the real stuff, I love the romance of the first courting period, all that kind of stuff appeals to me. I think I felt that if somebody liked me, then I was supposed to [have sex]. I didn't realise I had a choice in the matter. If they liked me, even if they were a complete asshole, I thought that I had to sleep with them! It was another way of getting attention. I think that people really didn't find me attractive.'

She went on to say: 'I guess I felt comfortable in that relationship because I felt dirty and grungy and angry. I used to not like myself. I spent time overweight, underweight, wearing black, hiding.' This was not a happy time: 'I didn't really enjoy it [sex]. I don't think I enjoyed it back then at all. When did I start enjoying sex? Umm . . . for a long time I felt it was something I had to do, and it wasn't really a place where I could be free and experiment and enjoy. It was something that one did, you know. So I think it wasn't until I was about 22 that I started to realise that "Hey, I can enjoy this." '

> *Perfect: No one can know my elation. No one can know my situation. No one can know of my relations, perfect.*
> Entry in Gillian Anderson's Graduation Yearbook, written by her boyfriend.

With such unstable surroundings, Gillian's school work inevitably suffered. Her grades plummeted and she became a problem student. Indeed, one year she was voted as 'The Person Most Likely To Be A Loser'. She was a regular in the principal's office, for a variety of harmless but delinquent misdemeanours (perhaps the most stylish was hiding some pig's eyes in her teacher's drawer), and was a habitual truant. Even on her graduation night in 1986 she couldn't resist: she got wildly drunk and broke into the school in a vain attempt to glue all the locks shut. Caught fumbling around the dark building, she was taken to the nearest police station, where she was thrown in with the local drunks, winos and criminals. Her bohemian boyfriend came by several hours later and bailed her out.

Her sense of displacement and anger at being moved from London was only one contributing factor to Gillian's discontent. Another element which exacerbated the unease was the arrival in quick succession of two younger siblings, Aaron and Zoe. For years she had been an only child, and now that she was in need of more help and attention there were suddenly two new rivals vying for this. Gillian was not pleased, as she told the *Radio Times*: 'I was very jealous. I'd been the centre of their world, and all of a sudden I wasn't. I became a big, big sister at a time when a child needs as much attention as possible. I was going through puberty. I needed to find out who I was and to express myself in some way.'

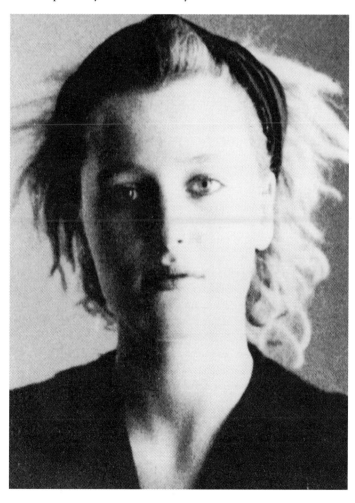

Gillian's entry in the Graduation Yearbook.

It is interesting that despite all this worrying behaviour, her parents let her go through it relatively unscolded, and did not force their views on her. Her mother admitted to being uneasy, but not frantic with anxiety, about this volatile phase of her daughter's life: 'Her anger over the move, and frustration with all the changes, were partly responsible for her turbulent years. She definitely had a chip on her shoulder when we brought her back to America. It was the last thing she wanted to do. But a lot of it was just a part of growing up . . . Gillian learned to portray a whole range of emotions by going through her problems and it helped her grow. To be honest, though, I don't remember her being quite as wild as she says she was. Gillian was a wonderful, sweet child and after she got over her growing-up problems, she became a wonderful, sweet adult.'

Looking back on this phase now, after her life took such a different turn, Gillian is quite philosophical. Although she acknowledges and remembers her unhappiness, she feels that it served a very important purpose in her development. As she told *TV Week*: 'There was a certain feeling of displacement. Moving into such a small town after growing up in London gave me a feeling of powerlessness, and it was a rebellious stage that I went through and needed to go through. I think back on it now and feel like it was a statement to myself. It was a feeling of power, saying something instead of nothing, that was necessary for me to go through as a stage in my life.

'I think on the whole it made me a more independent and a stronger person. Even though it was a crutch, so to speak, at times.' And she conceded: 'Life was excruciatingly painful for years. I'd deal with it by being quite wild – promiscuous, drinking a lot. Anything and everything was fair game. Ninety-nine per cent of students do exactly the same, so why should I be any different? Some get caught up in it, and it doesn't stop. Fortunately I was lucky and came out the other side. Something inside me always knew what I wanted to accomplish in life, and I was influenced by some remarkable people who got me out of the situation I was in. I listened, received their support.'

Gillian also appears to subscribe to the rather clichéd school of the thought that admires the 'tortured bed-sit artiste', as revealed by this statement to the *Radio Times*: 'My parents were scared I'd get hurt or in trouble, but allowed me to be independent and do whatever I needed. Some things were hard for them. I'm not sorry. I needed to go through it, and they needed to deal with what they were experiencing with me. The best artists seem to be the ones who have had most turmoil in their lives.'

In later years when Gillian had become a global superstar, her rebel punk phase attracted much retrospective interest, particularly from the mainstream media who were horrified that such a nice young girl could have been such a reprobate. Gillian has seen these formative years dissected and blown out of all proportion to what they actually were, and has now dismissed them as 'just growing up' and 'boring'. However, they were undeniably important. In actual fact, despite not being the ideal situation for a young girl, this phase taught her several things. Firstly, she realised that she had an individuality and enjoyed displaying that; in her own words, 'it was only when I started to shave my head and dress differently that I realised I had a voice as to who I was and what I stood for'.

Secondly, her strange accent meant that whenever there was an English part up for grabs in the school drama productions, Gillian would get the role. Her mother remembers seeing something in the rebellious child even at this early stage, as she later told *Sunday* magazine: 'From the start Gillian had a real flair for the dramatic. That has simply always been her personality. The first time I knew something was really up with her and acting was when she was fourteen and a teacher assigned her the *Romeo and Juliet* balcony scene. Gillian had no background in Shakespeare, acting or anything remotely like it. Nobody on either side of our family had any experience with acting. Her father was interested in film production, but that had mostly been connected with industrial training films and commercials. But she studied that scene and mastered it with no effort whatever. When she performed it my jaw just dropped. I was incredibly impressed and knew then that she was going to be an actress.'

Since her school work had suffered during this period, the phase also had the unwitting benefit of introducing Gillian to even more acting. By the Eleventh Grade, she was so bored with school that she decided to go to an audition almost on a whim, at a local community play. She got the part and suddenly felt invigorated: 'It gave me an outlet to express myself, it was so freeing.' Within months, her new focus on acting had sharpened her drive, and she was now voted 'Most Improved Student'. The corner had been turned.

Thus Gillian started on the long path towards global fame with *The X-Files*. Meanwhile, her punk drop-out boyfriend had gone on to become a showbiz lawyer, a job which Gillian felt perfectly suited his character of 'a pathological liar'. Still, he can't be any worse at that than he is at poetry.

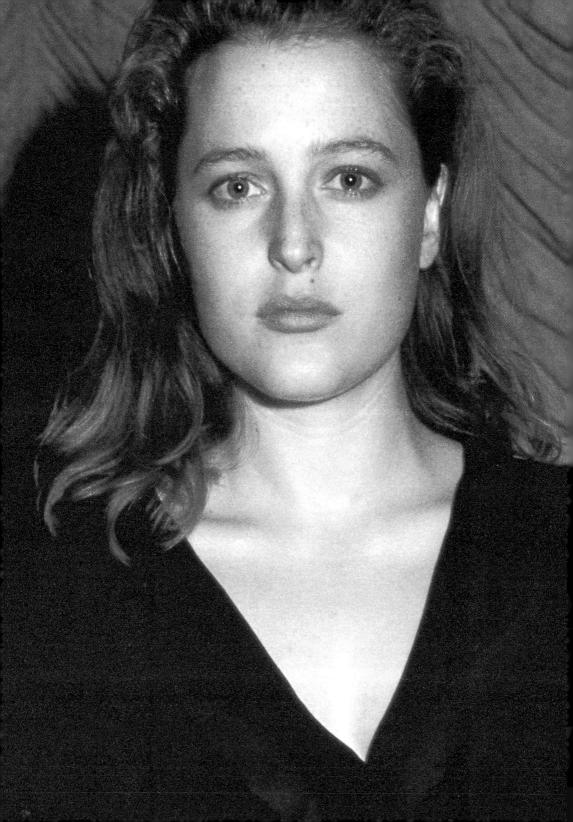

THE TURNING: GILLAN MOVES

Gillian's early ambition for when she was 'a grown-up' was to be a marine biologist, so it is an indication of the instant attraction of acting that she changed career paths so dramatically. Her involvement in the community theatre had such a profound effect that her earlier, scientific aspirations were immediately forgotten, and she became determined to pursue acting professionally.

On graduation, rather than resuming the drop-out lifestyle full-time, as many would have predicted for her, Gillian moved to Chicago where she enrolled at The Goodman Theater School at De Paul University, on a theatre studies course. The institution was a major theatre conservatory that had joined forces with De Paul University for academic purposes. Gillian has since been very protective of any stories from this period, but it is clear that she was still struggling with the inflammable lifestyle of her earlier, teenage years. Drink was clearly a major presence. When asked by *FHM* if she was abusing the drink, the now predominantly teetotal (since her twenty-first birthday) Gillian elaborates: 'I actually like alcohol a bit too much. I gave up because it was becoming . . . it was just getting too much, I just realised that all I wanted to do was drink. [When drunk] I was very introverted. It would've been fine after the first three drinks if everybody just left. But also it was a sexual stimulant for me. It made me feel much stronger and more confident and sexier and I relied on that for a while. [I drank] too much. But that's another story and I don't want to talk about it.'

It was during this period that her parents' liberal attitude began to pay dividends. Although Gillian was still unstable, her new focus on acting matured her and she was able to grow in confidence and start to become self-sufficient. This revitalised interest and motivation was shown by her decision to attend a summer acting school after normal term in 1988 at The National Theater of Great Britain, at Cornell University in Ithaca. Of the various roles she played during this period, her favourite was as a French maid in a farce called *A Flea In Her Ear*, which she enjoyed because 'it was good for me to explore the comedic side of acting'.

Gillian's attention turned to acting just before graduation, and the new focus gave her an intense sense of direction.

By 1990 Gillian had graduated from the four-year University course. As with many theatre schools, a graduation tour was arranged whereby the successful students performed on tour in front of an audience of agents, managers, scouts and industry people. When a representative from William Morris, America's most powerful acting agency, watched Gillian's monologue during one of the dates of this tour, he was impressed enough to immediately offer to represent her. One of her teachers at the time, Ric Murphy, recalls that the agent was not alone in his admiration of her talent: 'Being with Gillian was like going to a surprise party, she had an eight-line part in that French farce, but turned it into a star role just by the attitude she brought to it. She has an incandescence.' The William Morris scout agreed: he offered to take her on their books, but only on the condition that she re-locate to New York immediately.

So, with her Bachelor of Fine Arts degree rolled up in her bag, and her entire life's possessions shoved into the back of her VWRabbit, Gillian uprooted once more and headed out at 11 o' clock one night for the Big Apple. 'I had it in my mind that I should leave on a certain day, but it took longer to pack than I expected. The car was packed so high that I couldn't see out the rear-view mirror, and when I stopped to sleep, I had to crouch up in a fetal position.' Despite her apparent willingness to up-sticks at the first scent of a lucky break, one thing she was determined not to do was 'sell out'. That night, as she slept curled up in her car halfway along the journey, she made two vows: firstly, that she would never move to Los Angeles and secondly that she would never do television. Yeah, right.

Places like Los Angeles and New York are a strange paradox – they succeed both in fuelling and destroying people's dreams at the same time. Within days of Gillian Anderson arriving in New York, she had realised that despite her bullish agency backing, decent (indeed, any) roles were not going to be easy to find. She got a couple of corny advert jobs which were shot but never broadcast, but little else; so, within a matter of weeks she was looking for the trusty old 'day job'. Like many great actresses before her, she took to waiting on tables, at a student hang-out called Dojo in St Marks Place, Greenwich Village. She worked her shifts there around dozens of auditions, clocking up long hours of soul-destroying rejections and tiring café graft. Her hard work and perseverance appeared to have paid off in 1991, when she was offered the chance to audition for a role in an off-Broadway production of Allan Ayckbourne's *Absent Friends*, at the Manhattan Theater Club. The show had been in rehearsals for two weeks, but one of the key players, Mary-Louise Parker, had been offered a starring role in Lawrence Kasdan's *Grand Canyon* and had promptly left on the spot. Scores of actresses were auditioned and Gillian was finally offered the part.

The producers had chosen well – Gillian's performances were critically acclaimed, and she was subsequently awarded a prestigious Theater World Award for her efforts. With such an accolade under her belt, Gillian was one large step nearer to success. Once the play was over, however, she returned to waitress work, but was not too down-hearted as she recognised this was inevitable in the itinerant and unstable lifestyle she had chosen.

Gillian's determination and ambition kept her focused during the early days of auditions, rejections and waiting tables.

She continued ploughing fruitlessly through audition after audition until she was offered three key roles, all in the same period in 1992. With a sudden glut of work on offer, she chose to turn down another off-Broadway play in favour of a play in New Haven and a small feature-film role.

So it was that Gillian made her film debut in the low budget, soon-to-be-forgotten (then hastily remembered) *The Turning* (initially called *Home Fires Burning*). It was hailed as 'a dramatic story-line of love, alienation and violent racial bigotry in small-town America', but in reality was a low-cost, instantly forgettable flop, merely resurrected later because of Gillian's future celebrity. Playing alongside Tess Harper and Karen Allen, Gillian's role was as April Cavanaugh, a woman whose psychotic boyfriend returns to his home town, determined to wreak havoc on his family and his father's extra-marital relationship; April is left to pick up the emotional pieces after his absence of four years. Unlike the strait-laced Dana Scully, Gillian's character in *The Turning* shed the odd item of clothing as a love-starved waitress looking for excitement in a ghost town. The film never recouped and was a wholesale failure. Despite this, it was 'rush-released' in December 1996 to meet the huge demand for the footage that Gillian Anderson's fame had now created. The television network HBO showed questionable taste when they picked up the film and broadcast it, while Gillian did her best to put fans off buying the sorry affair.

With this poorly received, but admittedly invaluable experience under her belt, Gillian started work on the second of these new job offers, in *The Philanthropist*, a Christopher Hampton play based at The Long Wharf Theater in New Haven, Connecticut. Despite her growing experience, she still suffered from nerves, as she told writer Virginia Campbell: 'Oh, man. I've suffered life fright too, which I don't want to get into. Stage fright is very similar. I felt like somebody had shot crystal methedrine into my arm. It was physical – I was shaking, and I just wanted to get off the stage. I realised I had lines, but I was just going blank. Then autopilot took over.' Fortunately, stage fright was a rare occurrence for Gillian, and her work in *The Philanthropist* was critically applauded. She enjoyed working on the play and during her time there began to date one of her fellow actors, but that relationship soon finished when he moved to Los Angeles. At least Gillian had no intention of doing that.

When Gillian's boyfriend from *The Philanthropist* moved to LA, the young actress found herself once again in a dilemma. After a few days, her partner phoned and invited her to stay in his new home city, encouraging her with tales of how many roles were available, how producers were desperate for good actors. Gillian resolutely refused to relocate again, but was keen to see her boyfriend, so she bought a return ticket for a two-week visit. Once she arrived, all that changed: within three days, she had sold her return plane ticket, and was forced to rely on her generous boyfriend to support her while she tried desperately hard to get acting work.

When almost a year had passed without any results, it seemed that her brave decision had been rather foolhardy. She was attending three or four auditions a day, still with the help of the William Morris agency, but all to no avail. Then, towards the end of that first desolate year, she started to get a few breaks. Firstly, she landed a television role in *Class of 96*, a short-lived TV series, in an episode called 'The Accused'. She told the *Philadelphia Inquirer* how her initial snobbish attitude to television work had been softened by the mounting pile of bills and the medium's changing standards: 'I had no respect for television, the quality of the shows and the work. I actually never watch television, and don't own one.'

Unfortunately, Gillian's role in *Class of 96* was as short as the duration of the unfavoured series, so it was back to yet more day jobs and harassed auditions. She was then short-listed for the part of a fourteen-year-old fugitive, Carol Ann Fugate, in the controversial show about mass murderer Charles Starkweather, entitled *Murder in the Heartland*. In retrospect, this was probably just as well, but Gillian remembers how much this near-miss actually boosted her flagging morale and confidence: 'It was neat and inspiring, at a time when I wasn't getting much work, to be considered for a role like that.'

Thirdly, as a partial favour to a friend (who was a producer) she agreed to record the voice-over for an audio tape of Anne Rice's steamy novel *Exit To Eden*. She was paid much-needed cash to read the first half of the book, after which a male colleague would take over for the remainder. The two actors were given only two days to read the novel, but it wasn't until the day of the recording that each respective part required a variety of accents, including French and southern USA, as well as male and female. To use Gillian's own words, 'We sat in the studio for a couple of hours and just, you know, just "wung" it, even though that's not a word, is it?'

Even after this illuminating experience, Gillian's desperation did not lessen. Worse still, her unemployment allowance was due to run out. When the post arrived that day for the last cheque, there was also an appointment for yet another audition. The cover note said it was a new paranormal show based around the activities of two special agents in a rogue branch of the FBI. Gillian would attend, as she always did, but would it really come to anything?

THE X-FILES

'I already knew I had the part, so I was totally loose. This was my room, these were my people, this was my part. I was just fantastic. I wish I'd been that good when the cameras were rolling. So I played the scene in a kind of sarcastic way – much more sarcastic than it was written – and Gillian was just completely thrown by it. I was toying with this person, because Mulder doesn't really care whether she stays or goes. And she was shocked that anybody would talk to her that way. That's exactly how she should have reacted. It was perfect.'
David Duchovny (on that first *X-Files* audition)

David Duchovny was right to be so confident. Compared to Gillian Anderson, he was a veritable veteran of the large and small screen. The Princeton and Yale graduate had scores of roles under his belt. Alongside the bit parts in *Working Girl*, *Julia Has Two Lovers*, and his role as the transvestite FBI agent Denis/Denise Bryson in *Twin Peaks*, he had also appeared in the sex anthology *The Red Shoe Diaries*, *The Rapture*, and *Chaplin,* as well as a host of other television work. Then along came the audition for *The X-Files* pilot. Duchovny was interested but expected nothing more than a brief commitment, as he told *The X-Files Confidential* authors: 'I thought I could go to Vancouver for a month and get paid, and then go on to my next movie. After all, a show about extraterrestrials – no matter how well made – how many can you do?'

As Chris Carter told the same authors, Duchovny walked into the part: 'David read for the part and was perfect. We were obligated to give the network a choice of at least two actors, but we knew David was it from the start. He was just very, very right for the role.' There was a second actor put forward, but the network agreed on Duchovny immediately.

Things were not so simple for Dana Scully (named after the Dodgers announcer Vin Scully). For a start, Gillian was competing with actresses with far more experience, larger chests, longer, blonder hair and generally more sex appeal. Secondly, as a virtual unknown she was an unlikely winner. Thirdly, she turned up for the audition in oversized and drab clothes. She reflected on CBC's *Midday Show* how, ironically, this helped her get the part: 'I didn't have

any money, I didn't have any clothes other than vintage stuff, so I borrowed a
suit from a friend of mine. I don't know if she was bigger than me but she
looked very good in oversized suits and clothes, so I walked into the first
audition in a very oversized suit and looked somewhat "frumpy" in that way.
So that's how the Fox executives first saw me and it was hinted to me that
I come in with a little bit of a shorter skirt and something a little bit more
form-fitting, and I think I kinda took a middle ground there. But I think
ultimately it was Chris Carter who felt that I was speaking for the character
that he had written, and he really pushed for me to have the role.'

Carter was indeed, adamant that Gillian was the woman for the part.
'When she came into the room, I just knew she was Scully. She had an
intensity about her, the kind of intensity that translates well across the screen.'

Despite this, the Fox executives were utterly unconvinced. There were a
whole host of reasons why she shouldn't get the part, a total lack of suitable
experience being the major one. After all, what good is one episode of a failed
series? Carter stood his ground and insisted that she be given yet more
auditions. He won the day and so Gillian was hauled in front of the next
network audition for a grilling, alongside a selection of more curvaceous
blondes that Fox had specially flown in from New York for the part. Against
such opposition it is even more remarkable that this time Gillian won the job.
'What it came down to was that the network wasn't sure how Gillian would
look in a bathing suit, they didn't really know what the show was. There were
people who were very, very nervous about my insistence on casting her,'
remembers Carter. It was with some relief that she heard the news – this could
clear the mounting bills and rent cheques, for a few months at least.

Already at this stage Carter was aware that there seemed to be a definite
chemistry between Gillian and her opposite number, Duchovny, and this was
something that she noticed too – she well remembers her first meeting with
her future co-star: 'We hit it off straight away, we almost fell into a rhythm
while we were reading together and it felt really comfortable.' This was the
intangible element that Carter had spotted and the Fox people hadn't. It was
also the chemistry that, within a matter of eighteen months, would make
The X-Files one of the most successful television shows in the world.

Oh, and they didn't ask her if she believed in aliens.

It is easy to reflect on the global success of *The X-Files* and to think that
Duchovny and Anderson should have been ecstatic at being cast for the roles
of Mulder and Scully. However, back then it was far from that simple. For a
start, Duchovny was a hard-headed veteran, who knew the realities of a show
succeeding and suspected that an alien-based series was even less likely to

succeed than most. On the other hand, there was Gillian, who had absolutely no conception of what she was getting involved in, by her own admission: 'I didn't know what it entailed. I didn't even know what a pilot was,' she told *TV Week*, looking back with amusement on the audition that changed her life. 'I don't think I even cared whether it was going to get picked up or not, but once we did it and I started to know a little bit more about the whole TV thing, I was hoping we could just get picked up for a year or something like that.'

She admitted, too: 'You know, at the time, I had no idea what was going on. I was basically just doing what was put right in front of my nose, and I had no concept or idea of how long it would run or . . . I don't think at the time that I really even cared. I had a job, and somebody wanted me to act and I was happy with that, so I don't think I thought about it that much.' And finally: 'When I first starting auditioning for the show, I didn't understand what the odds were for a show to get picked up. I thought that all shows were picked up.'

Scully frequently liaises with an on-the-road Mulder from her laboratory.

One thing she did know, and that was that she liked the character of Dana 'Starbuck' Scully. When she got the script from her agent, she admitted that 'I couldn't put it down', and went on to say: 'I was reading something that for the first time in a long time involved a strong, independent, intelligent woman as a lead character.'

As a star recruit from the FBI, Scully's logic and sceptical approach provided an essential contrast to her partner's rather more fanciful investigative procedures.

Scully is an expert doctor and medical graduate, and joined the FBI as a star recruit. On taking her new post she was immediately posted to accompany the brilliant but slightly maverick agent, Fox Mulder, in his so-called 'X Files' investigations. These were cases that were deemed to be outside the normal scope of the Bureau. Agent Fox Mulder is one of the FBI's greatest detectives – his photographic memory and psychology expertise have helped him profile many serial killers. Scully is there to assist, but also to keep an eye on his manoeuvres, which are focused around his sister's alleged childhood abduction by aliens (his obsession with this led him to be nicknamed 'Spooky'). On his office wall he has the poster bearing the legend:'I want to believe.' As a scientific sceptic dealing in reality, Scully is there to ground his theories in fact. The dynamics between the two, and the cases they pursue, were to make up the crux of the show.

Filming was to be based in North Shore studios in Vancouver, also home to Fox's *Strange Luck*, an area picked because it was, as Carter says, 'the biggest film lot in the north-west'. Rather than locate in the traditional area of Los Angeles, the plan was to write the material at Twentieth Century's Studios down there, then have a production crew in Vancouver to translate the bizarre story-lines into reality. Each full script was turned into a virtual mini-movie in only eight days. On such a schedule, it immediately became apparent that this would be a life-dominating show. Gillian had to move up to Canada from Los Angeles, and within days realised that her life would never be the same again.

First to go was her hair style and colour. She had naturally wavy, ash-blonde hair that reached to the middle of her back, but Fox Network had the long strands cut into a now-famous sleek, strawberry-blonde bob, by Malcolm Marsden (who was immortalised as the British MP in the episode 'Fire'). Various designers were approached to supply Scully's clothes, including Armani, and they gave her a very stern, intellectual look, with both Mulder and Scully frequently donning long heavy raincoats.

Work started at 8 a.m. at the latest and Gillian was regularly still on set at 11 p.m., midnight, or even later. Indeed, the hectic, work-intensive tone of the production was set when Carter's team finished the pilot at 5 a.m. before showing it to the Fox executives, including the all-powerful Rupert Murdoch, at 8 a.m.

Episode 1.1 The X-Files, 10 September, 1993

The body of a young woman is found in woods near Oregon, but with no apparent cause of death – the FBI are called in as this is the fourth such incident in the very same high school class. Scully is given an insight into Mulder's psyche when he immediately assumes that, like his sister, the girls have all been abducted by extraterrestrials. Understanding his desire to believe, and hence hold a candle of hope for his missing sibling, Scully is nevertheless completely sceptical of his theories; until, that is, the cask containing the body of the girl is opened to reveal a malformed non-human corpse. There is a suggestion of local police conspiracies, and this is increased by a suspected arson attack and the disappearance of the strange body. The finger of suspicion points at the local Sheriff's comatose son. Along the way, they find only one piece of probable evidence – a minute metal cylinder that had been inserted up a victim's nose. This is handed over to a man known only as The Cigarette Smoking Man, who takes it back to a Pentagon warehouse.

'It's a goner.' Television critic on *The X-Files* pilot episode.

The pilot episode had all the features that would make *The X-Files* such a celebrated show: the open, undecided ending, the dark, taboo themes, the unsettling production values and frightening effects, the dichotomy between real and science fiction. And, of course, it was scary.

The pilot episode garnered generally good reviews, with Tony Scott in *Daily Variety* commenting: 'Looks like sci-fi/mystery fans have something they can sharpen their teeth on with this new series. If succeeding chapters can keep the pace, this well-produced entry could be this season's UFO high-flier.' Walt Belcher in the *Tampa Tribune* showed a perceptive eye for the fanatical following the programme could inspire, saying: 'This spooky drama . . . could be a hit. It's sure to develop a cult following at the least.' Noel Holsten in the *Minneapolis Star-Tribune* agreed: 'Not since Darren McGavin stumbled on to a different monster every week in *Kolchak* has there been a prime-time series as preposterous as *The X-Files*. Or as much fun!'

The constant high-brow discussion between Scully the realist and Mulder the believer is one of The X-Files' *central dynamics.*

However, ratings for the pilot were only average, and some critics doubted the programme had any longevity – Joyce Miller said in the *San Francisco Examiner:* 'The government cover-up is depicted with the right touch of paranoia . . . the problem is . . . *The X-Files* itself seems destined to end up in TV's archive of short-lived phenomena.' Fortunately as the series progressed and the episodes maintained the weird and stylish approach, the reviews got increasingly stronger. For example, Matt Roush in *USA Today*: 'File this under your "must see" heading: *X-Files* just keeps getting better. And weirder. And scarier.'

Within a matter of weeks, once the series proper had begun, it became clear that these were no ordinary scripts. In that first season there were stories of a body-changing, a human-liver-eating mutant, a Jersey beast who stalks human prey, telekinesis, parasitic worms that take over the brain with paranoid effects, extraterrestrial spirit possessions, clones, psychics and of course, UFOs. There were also the peculiar titles, such as 'Deep Throat', 'Conduit', 'Lazarus', 'EBE.', and 'Tooms'.

In the course of her lengthy spell on *The X-Files* Gillian would be required to do some pretty bizarre things, of which perhaps the two oddest were eating a chocolate cricket and fighting a stuffed cat. The former was during the episode called 'Humbug', in which a circus freak-show is investigated. A character called Conundrum, who is tattooed over his entire body in the shape of a jigsaw puzzle, eats some live crickets, and Scully rises to the challenge and swallows one too. The producers made a $1400 chocolate cricket for Gillian to eat on camera. However, she went further than that: 'There was this guy pouring a huge jar full of crickets into his mouth, they're crawling up his head and down his back, and and he offers me one, and I've got to take one out and put it in my mouth when he's eating hundreds of them in front of me. It was kind of a self-imposed challenge – but as soon as I turned my back from the camera I spat it out.'

The second odd scene was when Scully was fighting a crazed cat in the episode 'Teso Dos Bichos' – Gillian is allergic to cats' fur so the special-effects team made a dummy covered in rabbit fur: 'It was the stupidest thing I've ever done, three hours' worth of take after take of fighting and rolling around with this bunny-fur-covered cat on my face. The fur was coming off, going up my nose, and sticking to my lipstick. That was the worst.'

For now, the first season showed respectable, although not spectacular ratings. For Gillian Anderson, this was undoubtedly the most nerve-racking period of her career so far. Starring alongside a veteran actor as one half of a two-lead show, with virtually no television experience behind her, she struggled gravely with her confidence in that first year. Some might call it 'impostor syndrome', as she told the *Observer*: 'For a long time, there was this feeling that they were going to find out they'd made a really big mistake. Had it been a larger network than Fox they certainly would not have taken the risk.'

Added to her knowledge that Fox had wanted a blonde bimbo, her lack of confidence only reinforced her worries. Her audition had been so promising that she now felt under enormous pressure to deliver up to that standard. The exhausting hours and complicated scientific jargon that had to be delivered as second nature also exacerbated her tension.

Plus, the day-to-day mechanics of working in television were completely new to her, which she readily admits: 'I was a mess. It's taken me a while, and I'm still learning every single day I work.' She also said: 'I got the job when I was 24, so I was still in a period where I was desperately trying to figure out who I was, and working very hard at it.' She also acknowledged her inexperience and vouched for Duchovny's helpfulness: 'When we first started *X-Files*, I was so green. It was only my second time in front of a camera. I desperately needed someone to show me the ropes. And he did that. He was wonderful.'

As she got used to the hectic schedule, the problem of her acting being rushed became prevalent: 'On a daily basis, running through my mind are always things that personally I could have done better. But with this kind of schedule you just have to know that you've got to do better next time – let it go and move on. There's always little things that come up and make it more difficult.'

It is hard to imagine for a new show, but by halfway through the first series it was difficult to envisage anyone other than Gillian playing Scully – already the partnership between her and Duchovny was creating waves all over the television world. This was down to two factors. Firstly, the strangely natural yet brilliant on-screen chemistry between the two leads. Secondly, Gillian's rapid improvement mixed with her natural ability. On the first point, this acting dynamic is something that cannot be faked or trained – it just happened. At that first audition when Duchovny arrogantly scorned Gillian in between the lines of the script, her response was bolshy and perfect. He had done so from a mixture of his own actual self-confidence, and because he knew that the character of Mulder would have initially been extremely sceptical to be working with such a scientific cynic. In the event, Gillian's defensive reaction, in what was a tense audition, mirrored Scully's own sense of indignation – she was new to the job and nervous (like Gillian) but at the same time knew she was eminently capable.

Duchovny's early frustrations at Gillian's inexperience occasionally surfaced, but half-way through season one, she had come to grips with the role.

Even during that first meeting, the two actors adopted a monotone, flat delivery which seemed perfect for the characters, as Gillian told *The Midday Show*: 'I guess it was both of us, you know, exploring our characters, exploring the feel and the mood of the show as it was first starting, we kind of settled into that rhythm. I guess in knowing that we would have to investigate and react to so many different, unbelievable situations, that we kind of settled into this. We didn't want to take it too far all the time. And I don't think that it was a conscious thing that happened. I think, with feeling the mood of the show and how the characters were written, and the fact that we're exhausted half the time, it just kind of came out that way.'

By 1993, the partnership between Anderson and Duchovny was creating waves all over the television world.

Although Duchovny was helpful, there were times when he became frustrated with Gillian's naïvety, as David Nutter, one of the show's directors, recalled: 'In the beginning, she had trouble with her lines, and I think it kind of upset David because he is so accomplished. He's worked in feature films. He's worked with Brad Pitt. And he can learn his lines like that. But I know he appreciates how hard she works.' Exactly halfway through the first series, Gillian started to come to grips with the situation, and in the episode 'Beyond The Sea', when her character's father dies of a massive heart attack, she began to shine. Nutter was impressed: 'I was very moved and touched by her ability to be very honest, to tell the truth, in these emotional scenes.' This episode also represented something of a shift away from Mulder as the sole or main focus, which had been the case in the early episodes. Now, Gillian was starting to bring Scully much more on to a level playing field.

Gradually Duchovny's fears eroded as Gillian improved with each episode. As she did so, her confidence increased and the positive effect spiralled. By the end of the season, the duo of Mulder and Scully were inseparable. Duchovny clearly had great respect for his co-star. Describing something that happened in the pilot episode, he stated that they were standing under a rain machine in the freezing cold, trying to get the right effect. He was desperate to go home, but Gillian was having none of it: 'She's very tough, a survivor. She stood there wanting it to be colder and wetter. She was actually turning her face to the rain machine, saying, "Hit me with more water." '

By the end of that first season the show had become what is politely called a 'cult' hit. That equates to average-to-low audience ratings, with a load of 'weirdo' fans on the Internet, and big merchandise sales. Fortunately, this was enough of a positive response for Fox Network, who recommissioned a new series. For the traditionally tough Friday night slot, this was a great success (even though many fans admitted to taping the show while they were out and watching it on Saturday morning). What's more, Fox had been banking on another quasi-scientific series on the same night's schedule, called *The Adventures of Brisco County Jr.*, so *The X-Files* was something of a dark horse from the beginning. For Gillian, the personal repercussions of this success were to be mind-boggling. With this in mind, she had a new aim: 'I would love a tour of the Bureau headquarters. That's my New Year's resolution, to tour the FBI building.'

PIPER MARU:
HOW DID I GET HERE?

'I had a very good feeling that this show would be successful, but I don't think it's really even hit me yet. Once in a while I'll be driving down the street in Canada and think, "I'm in Canada. How did I get here?"'
Gillian Anderson

In the winter of 1993, Fox Network threw a party to celebrate the growing success of *The X-Files*. Among the guests crammed into the hall were a handful of psychics and paranormal experts specially brought in to add some flavour. Gillian Anderson sat down next to Debi Becker, a medium of substantial repute who turned to her and said, 'You're going to have a little girl.'

'How ludicrous,' thought Gillian. Firstly, she had no boyfriend; secondly, she had just landed her best-ever role in a show that appeared to have the potential to be huge, and thirdly, she had no intention of having children just yet. Still, it was a good party.

Two months later Gillian Anderson was pregnant with a baby girl.

It was still only a year since Gillian had been out of work. By the summer she had started *The X-Files*, and by the autumn she had met and fallen in love with a man who, two months later, would be her husband. Nine months after that and she would be a proud mother. Not bad for someone who was working sixteen-hour days, sometimes six days a week.

Obviously, under that intense work schedule, relations between people have to work well – and so it was on set that Gillian first met Clyde Klotz, a German-born art director who had joined *The X-Files* staff shortly after the pilot episode. He was a gentle and smiling man, well-respected by his colleagues and very genial. Gillian was attracted to him immediately, but says it wasn't love at first sight: 'No, it wasn't. I was very attracted to him, and assumed he was to me as well. We went out on a couple dates to feel it out – it wasn't bang or anything . . . I didn't faint.'

In tandem with the show's escalating popularity, Gillian's image changed noticeably from straight-laced FBI agent to burgeoning sex siren.

After their first date, when Gillian invited him into her trailer to eat sushi (cue millions of men world-wide rushing out to try the very same meal), the two got on famously. 'It was Clyde's smile that first attracted me. He was very quiet, rugged and cool, but I soon realised he had a lot to say and that he was a very intelligent man.' They started dating in September 1993, and within two months had gone through a whirlwind romance that resulted in his proposal of marriage. Clyde said: 'We felt like we'd known each other a long time, and we'd just finally met in person.' Gillian had, in fact, been engaged before, but she keeps the details sketchy: 'I had gotten engaged before, with a ring over a fancy dinner, and it was a very uncomfortable, thing, but this time it was so fabulously simple – it was just one of those channel-changing moments interrupted by wedding vows.'

The engagement lasted 'shorter than a month but longer than a week' until New Year's Day 1994, when they tied the knot, alone, and in a rather unusual location. Gillian sent a letter to her parents with strict instructions not to open it until January 1st, so it was just the happy couple and a Buddhist priest who performed the ceremony on the 17th hole of his local Kauai golf club. They were holidaying in Hawaii, and the priest felt that was the nicest spot to get hitched. Apart from getting married on a putting green, the two lovers admitted to looking out for UFOs: 'It was two o'clock in the morning and we were standing on this hill and it was kind of drizzling, and we both had to synchronise our eyes with the way the UFOs would eventually be moving . . . We stood there for God knows how long.' Two days later Gillian was back to dealing with fictional UFOs on *The X-Files* set.

While on honeymoon she got a tattoo on her inner right ankle – it was done in Tahiti by a heavily tattooed man called George, who, rather worryingly, used a home-made tattoo kit, comprising of a sewing needle, an old electric razor and a kebab stick plugged into a battery pack. The whole thing took just ten minutes. On set, Gillian's tattoo has to be covered up with sticking plaster.

When they returned they bought a three-bedroom house in Vancouver and settled down to married life. Straight away, though, they felt uncomfortable in their new home – they both felt uneasy, as if they were being watched, intruded upon. A friend recommended a Native American Indian who could cleanse houses of such forces. Open to this suggestion, the newly-weds called in the Indian, and since that visit the feeling has completely stopped.

If Gillian and her husband thought things might finally become a little simpler, there was more news to come. Shortly after their return to Vancouver, Gillian discovered she was pregnant. They worked out that it was as a result

Clyde Klotz' and Gillian's whirlwind romance culminated in a pseudo-Buddhist-golf-course-Hawaiian wedding.

of their wedding night intimacies. The shock was massive, and was a mixed blessing. They both wanted the child but their work situation, especially Gillian's, was very demanding. The show had just started gaining momentum, and now she was faced with a long lay-off. How would the staff react? How would Fox react? Should she keep the baby?

Clyde remembers it as a very difficult time, as he told *US Magazine*: 'We'd sit in silence and think, "Oh, my God, what could the repercussions be?" I imagine that all kinds of worst-case scenarios were flashing through Gillian's head, but she is not the type of person to verbalise them. She wouldn't want to tempt fate in that way.' All these and many other questions raced through their minds. Gillian reflected on this to *TV Week*: 'I knew the decision I had to make towards having a child, and I knew that I could also lose my job over it. I knew that if I didn't lose my job, I'd probably wish that I had, since I had to confront a lot of people about it.' She also went on to say, 'When I realised I was pregnant the reality hit me – was I going to lose this opportunity to work with such a splendid character and with the support of such great people? I also had a very strong trust that I should go ahead with the pregnancy and everything would be okay, no matter what the outcome was.'

This philosophical outlook was all very well, but Gillian was contracted to *The X-Files* and her pregnancy would involve major repercussions. Rather than going to the executives immediately, she first approached David Duchovny, to see how he reacted and how he felt the situation would best be played. His reaction was not encouraging – he was stunned. After a while, he composed himself and said that if she wanted the child then he was right behind her. That was a relief, but she still had to tell the boss, and ease his fears about her pregnancy affecting the show's chances.

Historically it was not a good sign. The once popular show *Beauty and the Beast* – starring the stunning Linda Hamilton – fell apart after the lead actress had a baby. One of the staff on that show, Howard Gordon, was now working on *The X-Files* and he was more than vocal regarding his reservations with this latest pregnancy. The series creator, Chris Carter, was either furious or understanding, depending on whose view you believe. One insider said: 'He went ballistic, he wanted to get rid of her.' Anderson herself heard rumours to that effect. Fox Executives were said to be furious that an actress who had been given such a break (moreover, initially against their wishes) now had the gall to have a child after the first successful series, involving re-casting and all the subsequent inconveniences – executives, don't you just love 'em?

However, Carter now denies he reacted like this, and says that he was prepared to stand by his woman all the way, as he recalled: 'I never, ever, considered replacing her. It's a lie. If anything, I was the loudest voice saying "We have to protect this show and this person." Scully and Mulder are two characters that the audience has invested in, they are the secret to the success of the show, and we have to find a way to make this work.' Gillian remembers he was completely taken aback, as she told *Starlog* magazine: 'Well, he was shocked. Understandably, I mean, everybody was. It was a huge risk, I think, for all of us to just go ahead with it. I don't think Chris was too happy about it.' Even so, he insisted eventually that they stay with her.

It was just as well they decided to work around it. Gillian could not see herself as a full-time mother, and was worried that the frustration of not pursuing her career would have repercussions in her relationship with the new baby. Even though the crew agreed to work around the situation, Clyde felt there would inevitably be a clash of interests, and so, shortly after the announcement, he left *The X-Files* crew. At first, he spent time carving a four-poster bed for their luxury home. He went on to work in films and then began designing shows for a company called Mainframe Entertainment, whose key show is a completely computer animated children's tale called *Reboot*.

'Yeah, my weight went up by fifty-two pounds. I packed it on there for a bit.'

Episode 1.24 The Erlenmeyer Flask

Dr Berube is a government scientist who comes under the beady eye of Mulder and Scully because of his apparent involvement in cloning extraterrestrial DNA by experimenting on terminally-ill humans. The two search for the truth with the help of their regular adviser, the mysterious Deep Throat. By the episode's finish, Deep Throat is killed, the evidence for that case destroyed and even more shockingly, The X-Files closed down (despite its higher than average Bureau clear-up rate of 75%), leaving Scully and Mulder to be reassigned.

One of the most remarkable elements of *The X-Files* is that each show is written and produced in just eight days. Because of this, Chris Carter knew that he could manoeuvre around Gillian's pregnancy, because the majority of the second season episodes had yet to be written. The way that the writing team manipulated the pregnancy to suit the show, and the incredible story-lines they produced because of it, meant that by the end of this second spell *The X-Files* was as innovative and compelling as any show on television.

Mulder is wearing a crucifix around his neck. It belongs to Scully, his partner, who has vanished with no explanation. She was initially abducted by Duane Barry, a mental hospital escapee, who has already taken several people hostage. Barry claims to have been in contact with aliens and is desperate to offer someone other than himself to sacrifice to the extraterrestrials. Mulder chases Barry and the captive Scully through a near-fatal tram chase, but when he finally tracks down Barry, Scully is gone. The X-Files are reopened.

Great ingenuity was shown by the production staff, after they decided not to write the heavily pregnant Gillian out of the show.

Once Gillian's pregnancy began to show it dramatically increased the script's need to cope with the situation. Creative camera-work was used to film shots of Scully from the neck up; from behind; sitting down, or doing an autopsy; using doubles for certain stunts and more often than not, with the now-famous raincoat swamping her tiny frame ('I wear raincoats about the same amount of time [as David] in the series, but it's actually me that gets the comments about it. Actually they're very necessary in the cold and wet of Vancouver, and I'm glad of them').

Considering the initial shock and the probable extra work-load for everyone, Gillian was fortunate in that the crew went out of their way to accommodate her increasing size and delicate physical condition. They frequently brought her chairs to sit on between takes, and found a large cot for her to sleep in when she was too tired. There was even a joke about the cameraman needing to buy a wide-angle lens. They looked after her once they knew she was pregnant, but she now recalls the in-between period when even she herself was not aware of the new baby inside her. One such episode involved Scully being shot and thrown backwards across a hard floor. Covered in protective body pads, she filmed take after take and repeatedly flung herself on to the ground, coming away from the set that night covered in bruises. Two weeks later she found out she had been pregnant during that scene.

Inevitably, as the birth approached, Scully's lines and footage had to be decreased since she was simply too pregnant either to cope or to be visually fitted in to shooting. Although hardly in a position to complain, Gillian was very frustrated by this development. She had just started to develop Scully's character and impose that notorious female presence on the show when Mulder was once again thrust into the spotlight and took the lead.

She recalled to the *Philadelphia Enquirer* how her pregnancy changed her behaviour and subsequently that of Scully's: 'There was a huge chunk that kind of shook things up when I was pregnant. Everything that happens to a woman's body when she becomes pregnant – the hormonal changes, your mood changes, your personality changes. I mean, I was a very different person. And I think Scully became a different person in a way during that time, too.' One of these hormonal changes was her desire, as is apparently common amongst pregnant women, to shave all her hair off. That was one development that the Fox executives, understandably, simply could not accommodate.

When the time came for Gillian to have the baby, Chris Carter refused to give her maternity leave. Instead, he had her abducted by aliens.

There was a large amount of blood being lost, and the screaming child appeared to be unable to break free. The masked experts standing around the woman were shaking their heads and watching, concerned. All manner of tubes and machines bleeped and surged in the cold, sterile room.

This was no episode of *The X-Files* – this was Gillian Anderson's labour. Although the process had started normally, the baby's head proved too large to exit the pelvis so an emergency caesarean had to be performed. Gillian was doped up on Tylenol and codeine for the major surgery. Luckily, all went well and along came Piper Maru Anderson, weighing in at a healthy 8lb 10oz, twelve days late. It was September 1994, just over a year since her parents had met.

Her father, being half-German, had come up with her unusual name whilst flicking through one of his old yearbooks. Her godfather was Chris Carter, creator of one of the world's most bizarre television series. Her mother was the lead role in that series. It would be an interesting childhood for the little half-Canadian, half-American Piper.

Having gone through such a difficult labour, with the completely unexpected caesarean, Gillian was bruised and battered but at least, she hoped, she could get some time off. She contacted the producers of the show to see about getting perhaps a month off. The reply came back: 'You're in the next script.'

Gillian's pregnancy had already produced some brilliant scenes. After her abduction by Duane Barry and the later unexplained disappearance, Mulder is left unaided to resolve matters in the episode entitled '3'. He is drawn to a case involving a series of slayings that appeared to replicate the Trinity Murders, a trio of maniacs with a passion for blood. During the course of his work, he finds himself irresistibly drawn towards the luscious female 'vampire' Kristen Kilar. Mulder becomes sexually involved with this lady, who in real life was his actual girlfriend Perrey Davies.

This story-line outraged the fans of the show, who swamped the Internet and *The X-Files* offices with complaints about Mulder's unfaithfulness to Scully so soon after her disappearance. Mulder then imagines Scully being experimented on by aliens who appear to have inflated her stomach to huge proportions; for this scene there were no special effects needed, as Gillian was by now eight months pregnant. It was a good episode, but inevitably the chemistry that the public had come to associate with the pair was missing. Mulder was lost without Scully, both in the script and in the production. The two were now inextricably linked.

The following show saw the return of Scully, in the second season's eighth episode, entitled 'One Breath'. She appears without explanation in a

Washington DC hospital, in a coma and apparently seriously ill on a life support system. Only Scully's late father's spirit pushes her back into the real world, whereafter she soon discovers that an incredible, advanced form of microchip has been implanted in her neck – possibly by government scientists experimenting with alien DNA, or possibly due to interplanetary invaders themselves.

In order to keep up with the schedules, Gillian took only a minuscule ten days off before she was back into the rigours of a sixteen-hour day. In this way, she was able to give birth and seamlessly slot back into the production, with little or no effect on the programme. Gillian was very impressed with the show's flexibility: 'It was pretty rough, but pretty easy at the same time. There were so many things I couldn't do and the camera couldn't do because there were only certain ways they could shoot me. But on the other hand, I think they did a fabulous job with what they had.'

Of those ten working days she missed for Piper's birth, six of those were spent in hospital, an extended stay due to the surprise caesarean. At least she was in a coma for the first show. In fact, she was so tired that during those scenes she actually fell asleep on several occasions – her stomach was still freshly scarred and blue from the caesarean, so little make-up was needed. In one take, she drifted off to sleep and could hear the actors around her saying their lines. However, due to only being half-awake, Gillian thought she could hear words in her dreams and so, hilariously, she replied out loud, ruining what had been an otherwise perfect take. She didn't have it so easy for the next episode, as she told *BC Woman*: 'It entailed a lot of running and jumping. It was physically difficult, and emotionally – well, I shed a lot of silent tears. It was horrible. There were plenty of times that all I wanted to do was quit and be with my baby. But then I would have had a lawsuit on my hands for breach of contract.'

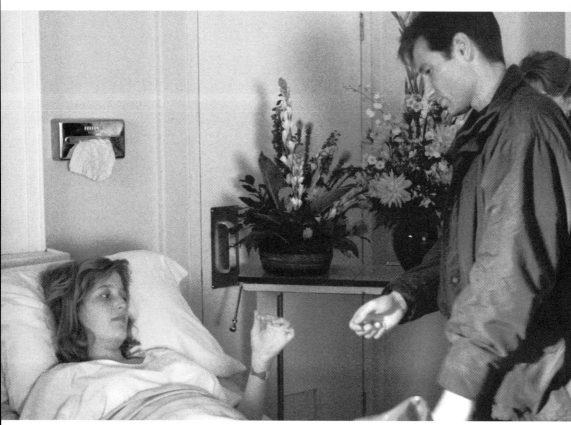

The abduction of Scully paved the way for Gillian's
brief maternity leave whilst enriching both plot lines and
developing the Scully-Mulder relationship considerably.

Moreover, her physical weariness from sleepless nights meant the odd artificial assistance was needed: 'The director of photography will go and whisper to the make-up artist, and when they come and start applying make-up under my eyes, I understand what he was whispering about. There's a general level of exhaustion that follows me around. It's a huge blessing whenever I get to make up sleep. I probably get about five hours' sleep a night, but with the schedule it ends up being pretty crazy.'

Despite these odd problems, the whole phase worked superbly and it is a tribute to the creativity of the crew and Gillian's hard work and strength to come back so quickly. Chris Carter later reflected, 'I'm very pleased with the way [the pregnancy] added to the show rather than took away from it.' Duchovny agreed, as he told *US Magazine*: 'The monster-of-the-week episodes are fun, but what makes the show really great are the extended stories, and I'm not sure if we would have discovered those otherwise. I think Gillian would agree.' Such creativity in the face of difficulty only increased the pressure Gillian applies to herself, however: 'The writers did so much to accommodate the situation, and the fact it's doing so well now added to the pressures for me to come back.'

Now that Gillian was back at work it was vital that she could tend to her new baby's needs, and the work would have to fit in around that. Fortunately the $30,000 per episode she was earning more than covered even the most expensive nanny, so Piper was brought on set with her mother every day – this was particularly vital as Gillian had chosen to breast-feed. During an Internet IRC chat, Gillian spoke of how she fits it all in: 'I do get to bring Piper with me every day, that's something I'm incredibly blessed to be able to do. What I usually do, if I have to leave really early in the morning is leave her at home with the nanny, and then I'll have somebody come and pick them up around two hours before lunch, and then she'll spend the rest of the day with me. Later on in the week, if I have to go to work much later she'll come with me at the beginning and then I send her home early so she can go to bed.'

Reactions to Piper on set were very positive. Obviously, as he was her godfather, Chris Carter was great, but he spent the majority of his time in Los Angeles with the writing team. Fortunately the rest of the production crew were very understanding of the immense pressure Gillian had placed upon herself: 'They were all very happy. There are many family people working on the show and they're all incredibly supportive anyway. They felt that I was making the right decision.' Piper would spend much of her early months cocooned in Gillian's large gun-metal grey metallic trailer with her nanny, leaving her celebrity mom to shoot in for a cuddle in between takes. They shared the trailer home with Cleo, Gillian's large neapolitan mastiff (which replaced a pet iguana she used to have), and the sounds of, amongst others, Alanis Morissette, Portishead, Counting Crows, Mozart, Miles Davis, and Dead Can Dance.

Initially they continued to use the stunt double that had replaced Gillian in her more tender pregnancy phases, as she was still physically weak after the birth. It was several months before she felt up to the full physical activity that some *X-Files* scenes demand: 'Much as I'd like to, my body is not back in the shape it was yet. Everything's a little off-balance, not aligned yet. Even walking up and down stairs, my knees can go out a bit. They've been careful about not making things too strenuous.'

Impressively, Gillian was keen to acknowledge the following that *The X-Files* was now gathering, and recognised her responsibility to that fan-base in California's *Telegram Tribune*: 'I'm incredibly fortunate to be involved in this series, and we're establishing such a following right now that [to leave] would have been selfish of me on such a humungous level, with the millions of people who are devoted to the show.'

Gillian was, amazingly, more worried about Clyde – her husband – than the enormous strains she was putting on herself. 'He's doing okay. It's a much greater shock for any husband. It's easier for the mother because you have all that time to prepare: your body prepares, your mind, your hormones. Men don't really have the preparation for sleep distraction that women do. But he's handling it very well. He loves her to death.' As for Piper: 'She has a wild personality and has adapted well to the situation.'

She also felt that Piper's arrival had given her a new sense of perspective, something which can be in short supply in the glamour-filled world of television: 'I am a much happier person now, nothing is quite as important since she came along.' She also claimed it made her more gutsy. 'I feel a lot stronger as a person now. I remember thinking, after going through the birthing process, that no cut, no knock to the head will ever make me whine again.' She also stated that she wanted more children, but wouldn't do so until *The X-Files* had finished, because the experience had been 'the hardest thing I have ever done'.

All the hard work, flexibility, creativity and mutual assistance worked – by the end of the superb second season *The X-Files* ratings were rocketing, and Fox had even started to use first season re-runs on a Sunday night to bolster that evening's figures. They appeared to be on the verge of something very big indeed.

*Gillian meticulously protected her daughter Piper's privacy from day one,
but her escalating fame and hectic work schedule meant she inevitably slipped
into the public eye.*

SUBVERSIVE

The X-Files, despite its massive popularity, its stash of awards and its leading stars' world-wide fame, is subversive television. What's more, it is subversive on several levels. Take for example the subject matter. Simultaneously the show covers horror, sci-fi, human freaks, evil criminals, extraterrestrial activity, government conspiracy; collecting up in one big bundle virtually every taboo in the book.

Episode Two of Season Four, entitled 'Home', is a good example of this taboo-breaking. The show begins with as chilling a start as mainstream television can get – the birth and subsequent live burial of a malformed baby. The story centres on a family who have inter-bred to such a degree over the centuries that they have become increasingly deformed and distant from the human race, as their unbalanced genetic mixture draws out the animalistic nature in subsequent generations. When the parents are supposedly involved in a horrific car accident they apparently disappear, leaving three sons in a house that hasn't changed since the American Civil War.

In the course of their investigations, Mulder and Scully are faced with savages, a booby-trapped house and other horrors, but the real terror is the incest at the base of it all. The show finishes with two deformed brothers dead, leaving the third son to climb out of the trunk of his car at the show's end, after once more planting his seed in his own mother's crippled and disfigured body. The credits roll as the incestuous couple drive off to start a new life with new children. You almost wonder if Chris Carter has somehow slipped these shows past the censor and the network executives. What other show could attempt this story and handle it with such taste? A sickening script, twisted into reality and yet remaining firmly rooted in horror.

There is the second reason why the show is such a success: the writing team assembled around Anderson and Duchovny is simply inspired. Each quasi-scientific yet unbelievable script is planted in reality, with both characters reacting in such a fashion that we *believe*. This is matched with what is essentially simple story-telling, which carries an age-old appeal, but done with genuine class. Only when the government conspiracies and running story-lines abound does the show sometimes become a little difficult to follow, and even then the more complex phases are frequently interjected with the popular 'monster-of the-week' episodes.

Unlike many other shows, *The X-Files* doesn't offer a regular solution – indeed, the scripts frequently offer more fresh questions than answers. Occasionally Scully's clinical mind is right and there is a serious scientific or at least human explanation to the mystery. More often than not, however, there are many unresolved problems or theories, tagged only with Mulder's wish to believe. Since the writers refuse to deliver a nice, clean answer to all the cases each week the degree of suspense never leaves the show. *The X-Files* fan goes to bed after each episode without a palatable answer – it remains strangely unsettling.

The continuing success of The X-Files *owes much to the conviction and believability with which Anderson and Duchovny play their characters.*

Unsettling too is the presentation. Aired at 9 p.m. in America and around that time elsewhere, the show is dark and eerie but not in any crass, Hammer House of Horror fashion. The monochrome filmic quality matches the monotone delivery of the two stars, and the lack of glamour is distinct. Scully, in particular, is the sharpest example of this – imagine Pamela Anderson flouncing around the US with Mulder in tow (okay, but really?). The dark grey wash that covers everything adds to the drama, a visual representation of the social disintegration focused on in the show. Even Mark Snow's famous theme-tune is minimalist and brooding. *The X-Files* is set very much in the real world, but is always visually on the edge of somewhere else. Hence, the show rejects many of Hollywood's most conventional tenets – glamour, love story (more of which later), cosy moralistic endings with easily understandable answers, Kodak-quality trimmed lawns and picture-perfect houses. It is infinitely superior to the majority of its rivals for that reason alone.

To add a nice twist to the proceedings, the humour is kept sparse and very dry. When it does arrive it is hilarious. Take Episode Three of Season Four, where the duo are investigating a mysterious African immigrant, who was born without a pituitary gland and is able to suck the pigment out of his victims by inserting a needle into their noses. In doing so, he leaves their black bodies totally devoid of pigment, white in death and horrific to look at. As Scully performs her regular autopsy over the chalky and rigid body of another victim, Mulder swans casually into the laboratory, glances over the body and, before he asks a single question, says: 'There's a Michael Jackson joke in here somewhere but I just can't find it . . .' Scully, without a flicker, continues in her vocal appraisal of the case. Another classic line is again delivered in the lab, when the duo are viewing the wafer-thin slices of a suspect's brain through a powerful microscope. Scully looks up and says, 'So what do we do?' to which Mulder, deadpan, replies: 'We get a slice to go.'

All these factors are highly appealing, but unless the show was grounded in a social environment that accepted such theories and ideas, all the production values and clever writing in the world would be lost. As it is, *The X-Files* came along at the perfect moment for such a show; with clear predecessors such as *The Night Stalker* and *The Prisoner*, paranormal and political conspiracy had already been heavily featured on television before. However, the social climate was now far more ready for such a show. With the new millennium fast approaching, the entire world has seen a massive upsurge in all things paranormal, spiritual beliefs, extraterrestrial interest and just about anything else connected to the kind of material dealt with by *The X-Files*.

It has been a long process, which began, arguably, when civilian pilot Kenneth Arnold sighted strange objects in the skies over Mount Rainier, and described his vision to the media as 'like flying saucers', inadvertently launching a modern myth. With the claims in 1947 that a UFO had crash-landed in Roswell, New Mexico and that the craft, along with an array of alien bodies, both alive and dead, had been captured, the extraterrestrial legend had truly been born. Obviously it goes back to time immemorial, with Greek gods, Romans and all manner of natural spirits, deities and suchlike.

However, the very modern twist which *The X-Files* gives the argument is at the core of its popularity. In the decades since Roswell, the subject of aliens and the paranormal has fluctuated in popularity, but generally it has remained rooted in the 'quack' world, drawing disbelieving glances and disparaging nods of sadness that people so sensible could lose it so much. In more recent years, there has been a gradual erosion of this perhaps understandable scepticism.

The ever-increasing numbers who claimed to have seen UFOs or undergone paranormal experiences started to sway the statistics. This general trend has been interspersed with various specific events along the way. Such as, for example, the celebrated and highly controversial work entitled *Abduction: Human Encounters With Aliens*, published in 1994. This infamous study was written by Professor John Mack, resident expert in psychiatry at the Harvard Medical School, and a writer held in such esteem that he had won the 1977 Pulitzer biography prize. His details of hundreds of alien abductions, and their alleged victims' accounts, caused uproar at Harvard and total fascination elsewhere in the believing world. According to his statistics, an incredible 3% of the American population felt they had been abducted by aliens – over ten million people! Mack was unsuccessfully investigated by the Harvard board of directors for reinforcing the unstable views of his patients, and no charges were brought.

Then, two years later, it is announced that rock samples which have been recovered from Mars indicate the sort of minerals that could, possibly, have enabled life to develop on that harsh planet. Add this to the myriad of stories, sightings and encounters and what you have is a massive library of evidence suggesting that someone, or something, may be out there.

Socio-politically as well, *The X-Files* could not have come along at a better time. Chris Carter himself was a Watergate kid, and the effect that had on his mind was substantial. Back in 1972, the Watergate crisis had raised in a serious and significant manner the possibility that the government was hiding nationally important things from the public. Nixon's attempts to besmirch the Democrats with underhand methods including burglary were exposed by Woodward and Bernstein, but the real disaster was the President's statement that 'there will be no whitewash at the Whitehouse'. The floodgates of disbelief and anger were really opened at the Watergate hearings, and Nixon's resignation was the final admission. In addition, the presence of the all-powerful, omnipotent J. Edgar Hoover at the head of the FBI meant that the entire government control issue was shrouded in mystery – his death in the early seventies, and the ensuing revelations of corruption, dealt a further blow to an already beleaguered FBI. Modern political paranoia had been born. With this new-found awareness, people began to trawl over recent history and dig up earlier conspiracies, e.g. flawed casualty rates in Vietnam. Even Kennedy's assassination was now open to all manner of theories blaming the Mafia, the FBI, Islam.

The trend was set to continue. The Reagan/Bush era only increased public suspicion of the central powers. The 'Iran-Contra Affair' enveloped Reagan and his Vice President/successor George Bush in a web of deceit and illegal arms sales to the so-called enemy of Islam and Iran. With the leader of the country floundering around for excuses and reasons, America and the world looked on with growing unease. With the Cold War assigned to the history books, events like these gave rise to the theory that the looming Soviet threat had been replaced by the 'enemy within'. This in turn spurred a rapid rise in militia groups and firearms possession in the USA. A true indication of just how suspicious the American people now are of their leaders is the fact that most would class an alien as less threatening than their own government.

In 'Humbug' Gillian ate chocolate crickets and is seen here talking to a man called Conundrum, part of a suspect travelling freak show community.

In Britain, this crisis was mirrored by the 'Arms To Iraq' affair, where a Coventry-based engineering firm's directors were on the verge of lengthy jail terms after making government-approved arms sales to Iraq. When the Gulf War broke out and the country was outraged at these sales, the government watched and declined to interfere as these innocent men faced prison. Since then, the BSE crisis over British beef has raised yet more serious questions about the trustworthiness of the British government. Incidents like these have

Mulder and Scully's quest to reveal the truth
behind government cover-up and deceit is one with
which the viewer can identify and admire.

been repeated all over the world, in every country in the last few decades. Arguably, such cover-ups have been present throughout time, but it is only as the media and society become more investigative, more demanding, that the truth gets out.

Mulder and Scully, as FBI mavericks, are fighting against this tide of government cover-ups. They are constantly chasing dead ends, red herrings, and are informed and misled by strange, ethereal figures who vanish into the night and go under creepy names such as Cigarette Smoking Man or Deep Throat. In a sense, they are the embodiment of the public, encompassing disbelievers, cynics and moles. We cheer them on and side with them at every turn. The poster in Mulder's office declaring 'I Want to Believe' is shadowed by the other great *X-Files* tenet 'The Truth Is Out There' – both of which the public aspire to.

As the public's suspicion of the powers-that-be increases, so does our championing of Scully and Mulder. The siege of Waco and the Oklahoma bombing are the more violent signs that members of the public are now passing through the suspicion stage on to something much more volatile. Maybe *The X-Files*, rather than arriving at a lucky time, arrived *because* of the time, very much a product of all these factors. Either way, it has enabled the show to become a worldwide phenomenon.

This increase in public suspicion has coincided with the phenomenal growth of the tabloid media. In recent decades, the tabloids have come to hold an immensely powerful role in public life. Woodward and Bernstein's superb investigative work was a major highlight, but there have been thousands of cases where tabloid pressure has unearthed all manner of scandals that would otherwise have gone unnoticed. To add to that, the tabloids' onus on sensationalism has fuelled the public's interest and belief in the paranormal. The *National Enquirer* carries headlines such as 'I married an alien' and 'My daughter is an alien', but behind the often tongue-in-cheek pieces there are people who are increasingly beginning to feel that this is not entirely impossible – hence the enormous circulation of publications like these. *The X-Files* addresses the role of the tabloids and effectively places many of their more bizarre stories on the small screen. The programme's rationale is that all these things can happen, and that matches the thoughts of the million-selling tabloids. They both appeal to the rubber-necking curiosity value, complemented by the age-old fascination with the darkest recesses of the human and non-human world, the combination of which has proved to have a massive commercial appeal.

In the episode 'The Host', Scully is apparently bereft of clues, when a tabloid newspaper is suddenly shoved under the door, offering an apparent solution to the otherwise dead-end case. Here the two similar worlds merge into one. *The X-Files'* recognition and ability to mirror tabloid ethics and beliefs is thus a major factor in the programme's success.

At the same time this means the programme is very much a snapshot of the 1990s. The tabloid sense of 'anything is possible' is ultra-modern, but that is matched by the end-of-the-millennium paraphernalia that surrounds the investigators, especially Scully. They both are lost without their mobile phones; when Mulder is entombed in a booby-trapped rail carriage with a possible alien being in the end car, and a hostile opponent threatening his life, it is completely acceptable that his phone rings (at least he can get reception in there). Scully is frequently seen in front of her lap-top or office computer, with the bizarre facts and details of research in progress scrolling down through the reflections in her glasses. Fax machines, ultra-intense microscopes, cyberspace, the latest digital circuitry, they are all here. *The X-Files* is a vehicle for the exponential curve of technology to be displayed – and it has a huge appeal.

Perhaps the biggest facet is that Mulder and Scully investigate aliens and the paranormal, but in the process they also reveal the frailties in humans. Paranormal activity frequently exposes a person's distress or trauma. Probably the biggest irony is that Scully, and especially Mulder, are the key aliens in the whole drama. Both are assigned to the FBI's basement freak-show cases, with Mulder's 'Spooky' tag being a dig at the waste of his phenomenally talented mind.

Furthermore, with the apparent lack of emotional or love lives, the two characters are very isolated. Scully's father and sister are dead. Mulder's sister was abducted (incidentally, she was watching the events of Watergate on television at the time), and his father is also dead. In many senses, all they have is each other and their work. Until Season Four's much debated 'Where's Scully?', 'She's on a date', and Mulder's liaison with a vampire in 'New Jersey Devil', the love elements were kept to the minimal. As Bruce Headlam said in his excellent essay in *Saturday Night Magazine*, 'When Mulder finally meets the aliens, you half-expect them to ask "What, don't you have a girlfriend? What's the matter with you?" '

'I trust no one but you, Scully.'

Which brings us to the most hotly debated aspect of the programme, and one which undoubtedly boosts ratings every week: the so-called 'Unresolved Sexual Tension' between Mulder and Scully. A television classic, a guaranteed winner, the unresolved relationship between the two has been the subject of probably more Internet space, and magazine column inches, than any other aspect of the show. *The X-Files* approach to this and to Scully/Anderson's gender itself is also unusual and a winning feature of the show – this will be discussed later.

Over the development of the series, the two colleagues have become inextricably bound together – Scully and Mulder go together as well as Lois and Clark, or Dave and Maddy. Unlike both of these duos, however, their relationship, as everyone who enjoys *The X-Files* must surely know by now, stands to remain unconsummated. Chris Carter is adamant about this: 'The show is very plot-driven . . . It's what I fought for from the beginning, which is, I didn't want this to be another *Moonlighting*. I didn't want the relationship [between Mulder and Scully] to come before the cases.'

Theirs is an epistemological rather than a sexual affair. They have so much respect for one another, they are so reliant on one another to even stay alive, that they are perhaps more close than a married couple. The trust and the bond between the two is huge and undeniable. Mulder is an occasional porn user and Scully has only had one as yet unextended date in four seasons. She had a supposed boyfriend, Ethan, in the pilot, but he was soon written out of the show. Gillian says this is something she would like to see opened up more: 'I think at some point it might be interesting to see her battle with [a relationship], not necessarily something that is successful, but something she is trying to work on at some point. It would be an interesting obstacle for her, but I don't think it's necessary.'

In addition to Gillian's curiosity, Duchovny allegedly threatened to go on strike unless some love interest was introduced into his role. So there is certainly room for involvement. There is the distinct possibility that both of them, at some point, have thought about being lovers. The occasional hands held, or face touched, helps to keep this unresolved tension simmering. Gillian thinks Fox Network should be grateful for what they inadvertently stumbled across: 'Not everyone has that chemistry together. It's not something that you can force. I think that Fox were very lucky to find two people who had just that.'

The on-screen chemistry between the two leads continues to tease and enthral X-Files *fans.*

Gillian also acknowledged, in *Starlog Magazine*, the appeal this element has for the viewers: 'I think people are intrigued by the relationship between Mulder and Scully and intrigued by the platonic professionalism and the sexual tension at the same time.' She went on to say in *TV Week:* 'I think Scully and Mulder love each other in such an intimate way without having to have sex. That is so obvious from week to week. It would be great to eventually see them have the greatest sex in the world, just as a relief for the whole audience, as well as them! We could have an entire hour devoted to just Mulder and Scully in bed together – with a half-hour of foreplay, and then raunchy sex with everything from handcuffs to chandeliers over our heads.' Er, probably not Gillian.

The whole point of *The X-Files* is the subject matter and not the love lives of the characters. There is no room for the added complication of romance between these two. What's more, the thousands of Gillian and David fans on the Internet would probably be distraught or delirious if the exchange occurred. If it were the latter, the suspense and tension would evaporate and, as with *Moonlighting*, the interest would wane.

All these factors and many more go into the melting pot that is *The X-Files* and have carved a niche into television history as one of the decade's most successful shows, as well as one of the most successful sci-fi shows of all time. Clearly, Gillian Anderson is central to that success, and her presence in many of the show's key factors is evident. Scully anchors the more unbelievable elements of the taboo subjects in reality – her intellectual and scientific approach means there is always a reasonable solution on offer, even if it is not the right one. If Mulder spills his coffee in a strange way, there are aliens involved, so without Scully's interjections the show would lapse into parody and cliché.

Her image and personal presentation are vital to the unglamourised feel of the show – as the lightning flashes across another dark plain, illuminating its scary secrets for a flash-point, Scully must not be seen adjusting her high heels or filing a nail. The monstrous overcoat used to cover her pregnancy helped in this staid workman-like appearance, and her monotone delivery of all manner of absurdly detailed scientific facts (with which Gillian readily admits she struggles) is perfect. She is almost a science robot at times; devoid of sexuality, emotion or prejudice. She cuts open the skin of another alien in the autopsy room with all the detachment of a man slicing cheese, concerned only to prove her theory that it will inevitably be a hoax. She talks of their internal organs matter of factly and offers solutions as such.

She has gradually evolved from the total cynic in the first series to someone who has been confronted by so much strange material that her reality-based ideas are inevitably eroded. As such, she represents the more suspicious public viewer, one who prefers to think these things are not real, but has to face the facts. At the same time, she wins us round by her intelligence and her willingness to believe against all her otherwise substantial knowledge. As a victim of a government cover-up when her sister is mistakenly assassinated instead of her, Scully is also someone whose emotional well-being has been shattered by these situations – just as a member of the public who claims to have been abducted by aliens is open to ridicule and subsequent trauma, then so too is Scully. She is, in theory, Mulder's minder, there to check on his investigations, but she cannot maintain this role for long, and her growing disbelief reflects the public's own disparaging trust of the government.

As the most technologically advanced of the two Scully is the show's techno wizard. She walks into a room and reads from a computer-generated DNA chart as if it were a children's book. When a tabloid newspaper is shoved under her door, she is already converted enough to read and consider its findings. And, of course, her role in the unresolved sexual tension is vital – perhaps more so than Mulder. She calls him Fox when his father dies, which no one else is allowed to do, but otherwise there is barely a flicker of romance in her eyes.

Gillian herself recognises these various elements, as she told *Starlog Magazine*: 'I think it's very timely right now. People are ready for this sort of show. There are many elements about *The X-Files* that are appealing. The scripts are really good and they lead people down an interesting path. We have a lot of money to spend, so the episodes look great, and we have an incredible crew. They just make it look fantastic and I think people really love the mood that comes across on screen.' As for government conspiracies, she is disgusted: 'I don't think it's the government's job to decide what people can or can't handle. People have a right to their fears, and learning to confront them can be quite liberating.

'Besides,' she adds, 'if there are life forms on other planets, travelling to Earth, they must be much more advanced than we are, which means we could be learning a lot from them. I think we should embrace that.' Add that to the seemingly colossal celebrity Gillian has attracted and she plays a central figure, not just in the actual scripts and story-lines, but in all these underlying factors that have contributed to making the most successful television show of its kind for years.

GOLDEN TIMES

By the end of Season Two, *The X-Files* had firmly established itself in the television calendar, now clearly transformed from cult status to mainstream hit. Although it came only in 64th position out of 141 shows in the category, this in itself represented a major coup for the crew and writers. Season Two's ratings were up over 50% on the first, and in some demographic groups, *The X-Files* ranked first in its time slot. Whereas during Season One the show had been compared to *The Twilight Zone* and *Twin Peaks,* by the end of Season Two other newer shows, such as *The Kindred*, were being compared to *The X-Files*. Also, whilst the FBI had refused to assist Carter in any form for his research on the project before the pilot was screened, the creator was now swamped with phone calls from actual FBI agents who were fans of the show and who inevitably managed to clarify a few details. In addition, Duchovny, Gillian and Carter were soon to be taken on a red-carpet tour of the actual FBI headquarters – J. Edgar Hoover would have turned in his grave. Things looked as if they could only get better.

It was not all roses for Gillian, however – there was a problem in her family that had been there for many years. Her younger brother Aaron suffers from the severely debilitating medical condition called neurofibromatosis, a neurological disease which can cause frequent tumours. Apart from the dangers of these being malignant, the tumours are often on the outside of the body as well as the inside, and can cause extensive disfiguring. Brain damage and neurological difficulties are also common symptoms. Neurofibromatosis, or NF, is rare and public awareness of the condition is very limited, so Gillian has become involved in educating people about the problem, and has openly used her fame and influence to help this cause.

Gillian told the *News of the World*'s *Sunday* magazine: 'It's been a big part of my parents' and my life for twelve years. It's been a major part of my growing up and Aaron's growing up because of the potential devastation of the disease.' She has devoted long hours to promoting the cause with her mother Rosemary, and between them, in their home state of Michigan they have founded a clinic for sufferers of the disorder. As well as treatment, education is the key, since one of the major difficulties is the frequent anti-social behaviour towards people who have the condition: 'I guess we want to make people aware that it's not contagious.' On one occasion Gillian and her mother attended a black tie event at the Whitehouse, to listen to a scientific discussion about NF. However, to a certain extent her job on *The X-Files* causes great frustration 'because of the hours involved, a show like this prohibits much volunteer activity beyond sending an autographed picture to a fund-raising auction'.

She continued: 'Aaron has been very, very lucky so far. Usually during puberty the disease grows rapidly, but he hasn't had that problem yet. Aaron has regular check-ups, and so far it's been relatively uneventful for him. Aaron is incredibly intelligent and athletic and beautiful.' She adds, 'His illness has certainly affected us in a strong way, and brought us much closer together as a family.' Her mother, Rosemary, is proud of Gillian's input: 'Fame had a good effect on Gillian. She's always been generous, and loves to lavish things on family and friends. Now she is loving being a position to do just that.'

Back on set, Gillian and *The X-Files* were escalating in popularity all the time. This fact was recognised at the highly prestigious Golden Globe awards in January 1995, where the show was nominated for Best Drama, and won; in the process beating off the likes of the highly successful *ER* and *NYPD Blue*. Even Tony Bennett, who was at the awards, announced he was a fan! Further to this, a whole host of acting, production and writing credits were to roll in over the next year or so as the programme's originality and brilliance was finally recognised.

Over the next eighteen months, *The X-Files* awards cabinet was also to fill with the following: Best TV Drama Series by the Environmental Media Awards for the episode 'Fearful Symmetry'; Outstanding Achievement Award by American Society of Cinematographers for John Bartley in the episode 'Duane Barry'. It was also nominated for scores of other awards, of which the most prestigious were the six Emmy nominations. Of these, they won five – most notably Outstanding Individual Achievement in Writing in a Dramatic Series, Graphics Design, and Theme Music (which was mirrored by similar nominations for editing, sound effects and cinematography). An Emmy nomination for sci-fi is in itself very rare, let alone a win. This was followed by nominations in the Quality Awards ceremony for Duchovny, Anderson and the show itself, and a nomination for an Edgar Award by the Mystery Writers of America.

Of this dazzling array of industry awards, it was perhaps the Golden Globes that did the most to bring *The X-Files* to the larger public's awareness. At the ceremony itself, Gillian and the rest of the crew were nervous, but utterly unconvinced they would win. Gillian was delighted to see Quentin

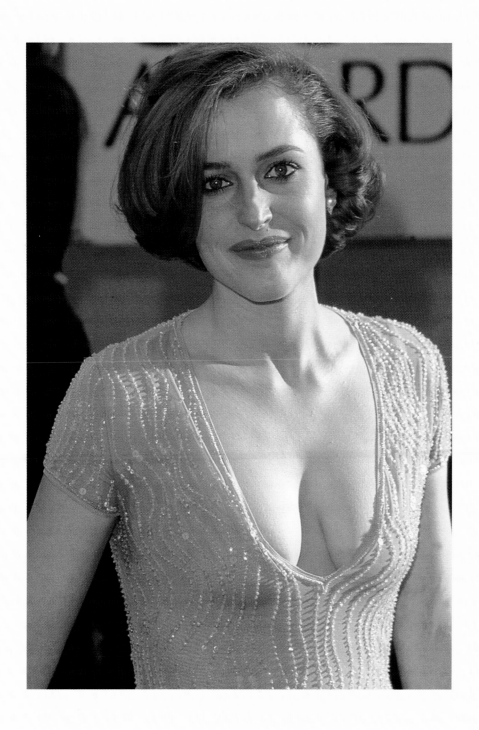

Tarantino there. She recalls: 'I was assuming because of the genres he likes that he would know *The X-Files,* so I walked up and said, "I just wanted to introduce myself." And he was polite, but he had no idea who I was, and, as he put it very eloquently onstage, he was "hammered".'

When the time came for *The X-Files* award nominations, there was total shock, as series hairdresser Malcolm Marrsden recalls: 'Did you see when we won the Golden Globes? Gillian stood up, and she was in an absolute daze. She just never expected it.' Anderson agrees: 'I had no clue about it. I just don't get it. And ultimately, I think that's good because it keeps my head small.' She still found it all a little unbelievable: 'At least once a week, I lie back in the bath and laugh at the ridiculousness of it all.'

Between this Golden Globe success in early 1995 and the astonishing five Emmy awards they won in 1996, the two lead *X-Files* characters found themselves experiencing the double-edged sword that is global fame. At first, as her star was clearly in the ascendancy, Gillian didn't suffer too much from the vagaries of international celebrity. Part of this was due to the fact that they filmed the show in Vancouver, not LA, and also because of the intense work schedule and her private, slightly reclusive manner. In British Columbia, the public were much more reserved, rarely accosting her in the street or hanging around the film set, although the occasional street location would attract a few prying eyes.

Generally Gillian was happy with this approach: 'They're very calm . . . I haven't been accosted by anyone. Everyone has been very polite. I haven't felt uncomfortable at any given time.' She had to start visiting LA occasionally for promotional work, and while there she noticed a distinct difference in attitude which she didn't like: 'I notice it when I come here, but Los Angeles is such a vast place and I'm literally shocked when

The show's success at the Golden Globe Awards marked the final ascent to the pinnacle of world television success.

somebody turns around and stares at me, because I forget why they would look at me! In Vancouver, I don't come across it as often . . . when we shoot on the streets, that's still only my real contact with fans.'

With Piper now a toddler, Gillian found that what little time she had left at the end of each day or week was spent with the family. This meant there was little room for socialising with the crew – Duchovny included – or for media work. This led to rumours that Duchovny and Gillian hated each other, that they simply cannot bear to be near each other once the cameras are switched off. These rumours were exacerbated by the fact that at first Duchovny got all the major interviews and big television chat shows, whilst Gillian was left to rummage around with the lesser known celebrities and programmes. The emphasis of the relationship then shifted when Gillian's celebrity started to grow and Duchovny found himself with less attention than he was used to.

Hence, the atmosphere between the two was generally reported to be less than warm. Duchovny has never fuelled this theory, as this extract from an interview with Deborah Starr Seibel shows: 'We are very wary of the fact that at any moment the other can turn into a psychotic human being because of the demands that are put on us, the sixteen-hour days. So I know when she is very tired and irritable, and she knows the same about me. We have a great respect for the fine line the other is walking all the time.' He also said: 'We don't spend any time together off the set, so we don't have a relationship off the set. It's not because I don't like her. I just don't want to see anybody from work.' Gillian reacted by saying: 'The first two years on the show were so completely about coping with this new monster that David and I didn't nurture our relationship, but we seem to be putting more attention towards that.'

Although clearly not bosom buddies, the rumours of star clashes is an exaggeration that Gillian laughs at (although the guarded manner in which they both answer these questions suggests there may be some truth in these words): 'It's a lot of work to be with someone as intensely as we do on a daily basis. Our relationship shifts and changes, and on the weekends we don't hang out because we're sick of seeing each other all week.'

Of course, the increase in salary and celebrity does not come without cost. Even though it was still less than two years since Gillian had been waiting at students' tables, she was already uncomfortable with many aspects of her new life. A very private person, she was particularly perturbed to find a British tabloid reporter arriving unannounced in Grand Rapids to start digging into her past, as her mother recalled in the *Washington Post*: 'It was pouring with rain, and this reporter came charging up. My girlfriend was in the driveway and she practically pushed her out of the way, and said, "I'm from London and I'd like to interview you about Gillian and her childhood and have some pictures and use some of your time."' The reporter

Critical acclaim and awards by the dozen continued their rollercoaster success.

then booked into a local hotel and started speaking to everyone in the town who had ever met Gillian. In an attempt to stop this, the family refused to talk to her, and told their friends to do the same, whilst Gillian went off on a vacation in Italy with her mother and Piper, after first doing a publicity stint in Milan – Clyde was to join them later.

This was a worrying development for Gillian and her young family. The invasion of her privacy was only just beginning and to make matters worse, the pressure on the show to produce better and better episodes each week meant that the hours were getting longer. Sixteen-hour days were now a regular, rather than occasional feature of her week. Inevitably, time with her husband and child was sparse. Her initial eagerness to respond to all her fan mail was now an impracticality, both in terms of time and the sheer volume of mail, but fame being such a recent phenomenon for Gillian, this was still something which made her feel immensely guilty. She tried not to listen to the tales of *X-Files* mugs being sold as quickly as the shops could lay them out on the shelves, and behind her laugh about an Agent Scully doll, there was a twinkle of concern about where this whirlwind would take her and what effect it would have on her life. She also began to realise that the show's success meant she may be trapped in this cycle for some time to come.

'I don't think it's hit me yet, to be honest,' she laughed as she told *SFX* magazine, 'well, I did think when we started work on Season Two that perhaps this thing might be going on for a while, because it seemed to be the only Fox show that was doing any good. We had a feeling we might be caught up in this for the long haul.'

The massive hours also started to invade her professional integrity, and she found herself being frustrated at the lack of time to work on scripts, telling the *Philadelphia Enquirer*: 'We work anywhere from twelve to sixteen hours a day, five days a week. I wouldn't wish it on anybody. But it's also the most wonderful thing, to have the opportunity to not only work on a specific character in detail, but to really explore yourself every day.' Even so, Chris Carter's writing team and his original vision meant there was little room for ad-libbing or flexibility within the script: 'There's a specific formula that seems to work and that they've been writing by for some time. It's basically given that when we get the scripts that that's what we do. There isn't really any time to do improvisation or anything.' She continues in *Starlog Magazine*: 'Once in a while, a really good script comes along that deals more with what drives her and Mulder emotionally and psychologically. And they're the ones that are more challenging to work on, and, ultimately, the ones that make the best shows – things like "Beyond the Sea", and "Irresistible".'

*The global celebrity she now enjoyed soon proved to be
a double-edged sword for Gillian.*

As a result of all this pressure and work, the Gillian that people read in interviews or saw on television at this time was not the bubbly and vivacious character that the public had become used to – she was beleaguered and tired. Asked by one reporter what fame meant to her, she replied, 'Suffocation.' To another prying microphone from Sydney's *Sunday Telegraph*, she continued: 'When I think of fame I think of the Catch-22 nature of it, I think of the benefit and the desire to be recognised for one's work and respected within the community and that's about where the line has to be drawn for me.' She also said: 'Fame at the moment feels like a lot of hard work.'

Amazingly, she chose to add to that workload by filming a new show in the hiatus. *Future Fantastic* was a nine-part science-based series produced by the BBC, which investigated the science fact behind the science fiction, and looked forward to the next century where anything is possible. Clearly closely linked to much of *The X-Files* material, it was Gillian's first major presenter role and she took to the task easily. She also thoroughly enjoyed this break from *The X-Files*: 'Fascinating stuff. It's highly possible, not necessarily probable. Smart people from every walk of life talk about their experiences with UFOs. I believe in them. It makes perfect sense the government would cover up, because it indicates there is something more powerful out there.' She also said, 'I'm really excited about presenting this show.'

The show covered such subjects as time travel, robots and, of course, extraterrestrials. Brought to production by the team behind *Tomorrow's World*, it looked back over the century's sci-fi predictions that became fact, and looked forward to what might happen in the future. 'Gillian is the natural choice to present *Future Fantastic*,' said executive producer Edward Briffa. 'If you're already dazzled by the pace of progress today, you'll be truly amazed and astounded by the promises of tomorrow.'

Of all the weird inventions and predictions on the show, Gillian was most taken with the possibility of transporting across the planet in a second: 'Wouldn't that be great? When you think of travelling, and the luggage and the baby and how long it all takes, it would be wonderful if you could just be there in the blink of an eye.' She also revealed that she had been offered this kind of material before: 'When I first started doing *The X-Files*, I was inundated by requests to do anything and everything to do with sci-fi and the paranormal, but I turned it all down, but *Future Fantastic* is different – it's being done from a comprehensive, intelligent perspective which just seems right.'

Future Fantastic *was a fascinating diversion for Gillian and took pressure away from her increasingly complex professional and social life.*

I AM NOT SPOCK

'I am not Spock'
Leonard Nimoy

'If people did think that I am like Scully, because she's such a fabulous human being and that's why they love me, then great!'
Gillian Anderson

Gillian Anderson is beautiful (English)
Gillian Anderson is mooi (Dutch)
Gillian Anderson on kaunis (Finnish)
Gillian Anderson gyönyörû (Hungarian)
Gillian Anderson yafa meod (Hebrew)

The problem is that people don't think Gillian Anderson is *like* Dana Scully – many people think she *is* Dana Scully. Not literally, not physically, of course. However, the blurred edge between Dana Scully and Gillian is such that the enormous fandom surrounding her is largely a result of the character on screen. Gillian's strong sense of privacy and her lack of lengthy, revealing interviews is a factor that exacerbates this dilemma, but it is essentially one that evolves from the fact that each week the public sees Scully and not Anderson. As such, Gillian/Dana has become a role model for a generation, a sex symbol for others, and has been able to twist the mixed personae to her advantage in the labour market.

Yet, essentially the two characters are hardly alike. It is worth looking at Dana Scully's background in some depth to discover why this character, and Gillian's role in it, has attracted such attention. Dana Katherine Scully MD is eight years older than Gillian, born on 23 February 1960; the daughter of a US Navy captain, William Scully, and his wife, Margaret. Her childhood, like Gillian's, revolved around her father's work, and she spent much of her growing-up years in various air-bases, including Miramar Naval Air Base, just north of San Diego. Raised as a Catholic, Scully is now rather lapsed in her practices. Her mother gave her a crucifix as a child, which Scully still wears, but this is done more as a source of pride and inspiration rather than as a religious symbol: the same crucifix that Mulder wore, touchingly, when Scully was abducted. Having said that, her strongly scientific background is increasingly being threatened by the daily occurrences at work, and the religious factor is slowly nudging its way back into her life.

Unlike Gillian, who is the eldest of three, Scully has an older brother, William Jr, a younger brother called Charles, and an older sister, Melissa. Tragically, Melissa was killed after being mistaken for Scully in the episode 'The Blessing Way'. Scully spent her first year of undergraduate school at the University of California in Berkeley, near the Alameda Naval Air Station where her father was stationed. She quickly proved to be highly academic, with an excellent memory. During her stay at the University she was involved in some political activism, including some anti-nuclear demonstrations, although she claims it never went past verbal discussions and handing out leaflets. This obviously clashed with her father's strict, fervently military ideas. After that fresher year, she transferred to the University of Maryland where her Physics graduate thesis, 'Einstein's Twin Paradox: A New Interpretation', was later published to some acclaim. She graduated with her medical degree in 1986. She also studied a residency in forensic pathology, hence her aptitude with the scalpel. She joined the FBI in 1990, straight out of medical school as one of a hand-picked group of high-achievers, but even this accolade disappointed her strict parents. However, in comparison with Gillian's turbulent childhood, Scully's was perhaps a model of study and application.

She enrolled at the FBI training academy as a high flyer, and immediately took to the new regime with impressive discipline. Socially, during this spell she became involved with an instructor named Jack Willis at the academy in Quantico, with whom she went out for over a year. Although the relationship ended on that level, they remained friends but Willis was tragically killed in the line of duty whilst investigating a case with Mulder and Scully. This coincided with another tragedy in the family in 1994, when Scully's father died of a huge coronary. Although they often clashed, Scully was close to her father, hence the pet names they gave to each other of Ahab and Starbuck (Scully), taken from the classic novel *Moby Dick*.

On arriving for active duty at the FBI in 1992, she was assigned by Section Chief Scott Blevins to be Special Agent Fox Mulder's partner-cum-minder, and to assess whether his obsessions with the so-called 'X Files' were justified. Initially, as the complete sceptic, Scully was convinced that there is a scientific or quasi-scientific explanation for everything, a theory in stark contrast to Agent Mulder's belief in all things extraordinary. However, over time she becomes embroiled in his obsessions and her resolute realism is chipped away. By May 1994, Assistant Director Skinner shuts down *The X-Files* (end of Season One), and reassigns both Mulder and Scully.

Scully is sent back to the Quantico Training Facility as an instructor. After further complications, she is abducted by Duane Barry in October of that year, but when he is cornered there is no sign of her. Mulder believes she has been abducted by aliens and is desperate to find her, having already lost his sister in this way. The following month, *The X-Files* are reopened and Scully reappears: on a life support system in the Intensive Care Unit of North Georgetown Hospital. On her full recovery she is reinstated to full and active duty. Since then, she has become more experienced and knowledgeable in her chosen field, and yet her scepticism is gradually eroding – she will never be as open as Mulder, but there has been a noticeable transition.

> *'At the same time that Scully reiterates the visible norms of femininity, she cites historically masculinised discourses as well.'* Lisa Parks

> *'She's a great-looking bird with nerves of steel.'* An Internet X Phile

Scully's character is highly appealing in many ways, and this is crucial to Gillian's celebrity – in looking at the complex reasons why Scully is so admired, it reveals much about Gillian's fame, and how this might affect her in the future. Scully is perhaps one of the coolest, strongest and most independent female characters ever to appear on television. She is highly intelligent, educated, fearless, and at times dominant in her relationship with Mulder. The absence of a cleavage and any sign of nudity separates her from the vast majority of female investigators on television, or indeed female characters in general. Take *Friends* for example, the massive US sitcom success – any coincidence that three stunning women live in the same block? Or what about *Baywatch* – the world's ten sexiest women all happen to work in the same lifeguard area. Then there's the new *Superman*, where Terry Hatcher's Lois is supposed to inspire feminine pride, but in fact adheres to many of the curvaceous, slightly hair-brained tenets so often seen in Hollywood. The nearest sci-fi phenomenon to *The X-Files* could perhaps be the phenomenal *Star Trek*. Here, however, there is a clear difference in the manner in which the female roles were cast. Female fans of the show were frequently frustrated, even angered, by the often blatant sexism prevalent in the *Star Trek* scripts. The only regular female character was the communications officer Uhura, but she was clearly subordinate to her male colleagues. Whilst *Star Trek's* morals and ethics aspired to be Utopian, the absence of a strong female lead in a strongly patriarchal show was a gaping omission. Even Kirk's women were usually fairly vacant but sexual creatures, and often in distress. Obviously, however, this did not stop *Star Trek* becoming the most successful sci-fi series of all time.

To be fair to *Star Trek*, times have changed. Back in the 60s when that show was made, sexual politics were very different. Since then, developments in contraception, abortion laws, equal opportunities legislation and the efforts of the 'Second Hand Wave' feminists of the 1970s, among other factors, have led to women having dramatically increased expectations, and a stronger identity separate from their previous roles of mother/wife/sex symbol. Scully (Anderson) reflects the more rounded image of a modern woman. A sharp, driven and dominant professional who nevertheless remains quintessentially female throughout. She is an image which female viewers in the 90s can more easily identify with and aspire to, rather than the clichéd, two-dimensional housewives of the 60s (Elizabeth Montgomery in *Bewitched*); the sex symbols of the 70s (Farah Fawcett in *Charlie's Angels*); or the hard-bitten, power-dressers of the 80s (the career-obsessed, mentally unstable Glenn Close in *Fatal Attraction*). Women in the 90s define themselves both in terms of their career and their gender – it is not an either/or situation, and Scully and Anderson both perfectly represent this.

This was highlighted very clearly in the early Season Four episode 'Home' (Gillian's favourite episode of this season), in what was one of *The X-Files'* most terrifying episodes to date. Scully's femininity was brought into focus through her discussion of the desire to reproduce, in the light of apparent in-bred mutations in an isolated family. Mulder comments that he had never visualised Scully as a mother before, but the viewer is never in any doubt that Scully is a woman.

In the same conversation, there is clear unresolved sexual tension when Scully states that we all have the impulse to procreate. Mulder replies, 'Do we?', and the question hangs in the air like a possible late night kiss. Scully does not reply – this is another key factor that makes her such an appealing character. In addition to the unusual appeal of her looks, Scully never disrobes, and her professional status is never compromised by emotional or physical love interest. In many senses, she appears very detached and cold, but it is unrealistic to expect an FBI agent of such huge calibre to have anything but a very focused and determined career bent. Scully is a character that separates herself from many of her television predecessors in this lack of unnecessary nudity and overt sexual presence.

For anyone similar to Scully, one has to look to the big screen, perhaps most particularly to Clarice Starling in the startlingly brilliant *Silence of the Lambs*. There we have an equally strong-minded FBI agent with an absent father, who is brave, highly skilled and fearless. Starling's father was killed during his job as a state trooper, and Scully's father is dead too – both aspire to make their late parent proud of them. Starling dissects a body with the same dispassionate objectivity and eagerness that Scully does, dispelling the faint-hearted, squeamish squeals of a thousand bimbo roles. Both are forensic pathology experts whose broad knowledge allows them to expand their work into many other areas. Both are petite, conservatively dressed, and relative newcomers who are learning on the job, in a patriarchal environment. There is even more similarity, suggested in an excellent essay by Rhonda Wilcox and J. P. Williams entitled '*The X-Files*, Liminality and Gender

Scully's unique blend of characteristics distinguishes her as a strong female role model.

Pleasure' (in the book *Deny All Knowledge – Reading The X-Files)*: the Starling/Lecter scenes in *Silence of the Lambs* are mirrored in the conversation between Scully and a possible clairvoyant in 'Beyond The Sea'. Both feel a degree of safety in their skill and knowledge, and yet are shocked when faced with extreme situations. Both are fearless – they will enter severely dangerous situations if the need arises, and alone. Both suspend the traditional gender stereotypes in favour of a much more modern, stronger vision. The writers for each respective character must be applauded; but, it has to be said, two such women out of thousands on television and film is not a good ratio.

Scully bends the traditional gender roles in television constantly. While Mulder is flying around bouncing off one crazy theory to the next, Scully is the stable partner, behind her computer or at the autopsy, anchoring the partnership to reality. Many *X-Files* fanatics have complained that Mulder is too often right, that his creative ideas on the extraordinary are often allowed to come to fruition, whereas Scully is usually wrong and this reinforces the

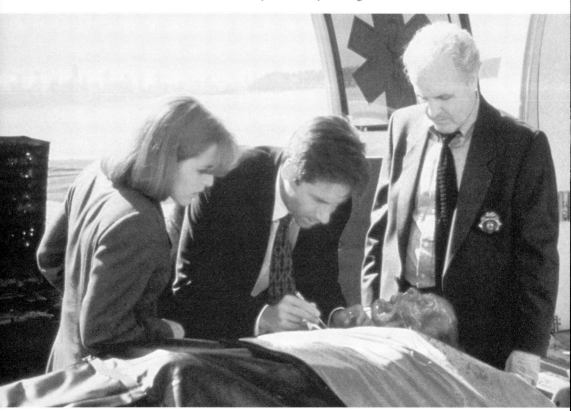

The character of Scully has matured since the early episodes with her taking a more prominent and independent role in the action.

male dominance. Mulder more often than not kills the bad guy, with Scully doing so only a handful of times (perhaps the best being in '2 Shy'). It was rare in the first two series that Scully ventured into a dangerous situation first; she usually tagged along a couple of paces behind Mulder. The notable exception to this was in 'Squeeze', when Scully was the first to venture down a darkened basement in search of a man who was capable of changing body shape at will. Elsewhere, the scripts sided with Mulder, a situation that was intensified when Gillian became pregnant and her physical condition did not allow for her to be in such positions on set. This definitely enervated her role for a while. However, since she has had the baby, her role has been more that of an equal.

In many ways the show is quite traditional, in that Mulder as the believer is the person the audience sides with; they want his hair-brained theories to prove the clinical Scully wrong. One empathises with him, and as such he is seen as the hero figure. As the show progressed, however, and Scully's character has solidified through Gillian's acting, she has become much stronger. Perhaps one should allow for the fact that she was an FBI novice early on and is gaining in confidence all the time. Perhaps, most importantly of all these matters, Scully is Mulder's *equal* – intellectually, and in terms of discipline, courage and endeavour: that is certainly a major breakthrough.

Another interesting factor in Scully's make-up is the way the producers do not use firearms to the extent that other shows have done with women. Traditionally over-emphasised as phallic, it is still true that many women detectives/agents/cops have seemingly been welded to a gun. Scully may use a gun in the show, but that is only occasionally; she is more often seen clutching a clipboard, a surgical mask or a mobile phone. Likewise, in publicity photos she is rarely seen armed – in fact, in the August 1995 issue of *Esquire* magazine, in a feature entitled 'Arresting Women We Love', there is a photo spread of eight women in police-related television roles, and the only one not clutching a firearm is Scully. Needless to say, Pamela Anderson in *Barb Wire* is armed up to the hilt.

As one reporter in *FHM* put it, Scully has become something of an 'Anti-Pammy'. Gillian is quite happy for this to be the case: 'I've been called "thinking man's crumpet", which is hysterical. But it's better than being called a bimbo, like Pamela Anderson, who is only famous for her body – if it is her body. I'd prefer to be known for something a little more worthwhile.' Now while most male readers would think Pamela's Anderson's body is perfectly worthwhile, she has a point. Most girls can't have a twenty-two inch waist, super-sized breasts and long flowing locks of blonde hair, but Scully has abilities and personal traits that they can at least *aspire* to.

As a result of all these admirable characteristics, Scully has become a strong role model for the nineties woman. The first inklings of this were on the Internet, where many chat rooms were filled with praise of her abilities, and *The X-Files'* rejection of stereotype. Indeed, one discussion group was actually entitled, 'I want to be like Scully when I grow up'. In that group, an undergraduate doctor taking her exams admitted openly that during the stressful few weeks of tests, she regularly thought of Scully as an inspiration for her study and concentration. Gillian has received bags of mail from young women, which delights her, even though they are clearly aspiring to be Scully: 'I've gotten quite a few letters from young girls saying I'm a role model, and this is probably one of the best compliments I could get as an actor. It's terrific because of what the character represents: honesty, justice, hard work and dedication and passion – and if that's what they're tapping into, that's fantastic.' She also said on CBC's *Midday* show: 'I think it was pretty early on that I began to get a hint that young girls, and actually girls of all ages, were considering Scully as a role model. And I just . . . I really enjoyed that and I thought that it was probably one of the most wonderful things that can happen, in that Scully is very intelligent, she went ahead with her education, she has a very moral mind-frame, she's honest, she's in pursuit of justice . . . you know . . . all these very positive, very strong elements and qualities in a female. And so I was very delighted to hear that women were responding to those attributes.'

An important point is that these are Scully's attributes. This is where the confusion arises over Scully/Anderson. The two characters are clearly very different, and it is the former who most people are familiar with. For example, at one Australian shopping centre appearance, many of the questions addressed to Gillian were actually asked of Scully. Such as the man who said, 'Those do not appear to be Scully's glasses you are wearing, are they?' Now obviously he knows this is not actually Scully (or at least, one hopes he does), but there seems to be a grey area between the two women. Gillian has even received mail forwarded from the actual FBI headquarters that has been addressed to Dana Scully. On a few occasions, people have approached her with stories of UFOs and close encounters, half-expecting her to dial the FBI HQ there and then on her mobile. She has also received hundreds of gifts and fan mail addressed to Scully, including a hilarious hillbilly song written especially for her, entitled: 'Oh Scully, When Will You Kiss Mulder?'

At one shopping mall appearance, Debbie Micallef, a mother of two young girls, attended the frantic event with her daughters because, as she told Sydney's *Sunday Telegraph*, she wanted to encourage them to be like Scully: 'It's good to see a strong female character in a TV show, she's a good role model for girls growing up, mainly because she shows women have a more important part to play in a man's world . . . I'd like my daughters to look up to her and Gillian as well.'

At least this hints at people accepting Gillian as well as Scully. This is fair as Gillian has, since her escalation to fame, been equally as hard-working as Scully and has achieved many things that other women admire. Obviously, being cast in the role of a successful major television show is a huge achievement in itself. So too is graduating from university. People have also liked Gillian's gutsy approach to the pregnancy, with the long working days and such an absurdly brief maternity leave, especially after a caesarean.

Another major factor has been Gillian's very public anger at the pay discrepancy between herself and her co-star David Duchovny. A tradition that is all but set in stone, Gillian was outraged to discover that her male counterpart was being paid ten times more per episode than she was. Naturally, the initial problem was that the executives would point out her inexperience compared to his veteran status. However, fairly early on (one could even argue by halfway through the first season), it was clear the GIllian was as vital to the show as Duchovny. Indeed, by the third season it was Gillian who was getting the most attention, and indeed an Emmy nomination, not Duchovny. So to continue to pay such vastly differing amounts was seen to be unacceptable. Gillian simply announced this point of view and that she wanted to renegotiate. There was talk of Fox re-casting her but that was never serious, merely shots across her bows to frighten her – it failed and she held out for a big pay rise: 'I think it sends a bad message to women and there shouldn't be any difference.' If the producers did not resolve the situation, she would go on strike. With world-wide syndication rights begging for more shows, and the colossal merchandise and money-making machine that had become *The X-Files* now at risk, the executives were over a barrel. She won, and received a substantial pay increase.

Gillian also used this conflict to protest about the treatment of women in the entertainment industry in general. She bemoaned the prejudice that is still prevalent, in *BC Woman* magazine: 'There are huge differences in the way male and female actors are perceived. Women have to be a certain size, in order to get good roles. The only successful, larger-than-average female actor I can think of is Kathy Bates. And once women reach a certain age, they can only expect one or two good roles per year, whereas male actors can continue working regularly well into their forties. Then there are the types of roles available to women,' she continues. 'We're constantly depicted as sidekicks, ingenues, and hangers-on, rarely as independent and capable individuals. And the enormous, huge discrepancies in pay . . . the amounts that some male actors make are astronomically obscene.' Aware that $30,000 is a lot of money per episode, her complaint is acknowledged as relative but still relevant: 'They'll never earn what their male counterparts are earning. Women in Hollywood are constantly shown that there's a difference between them and men, and that that's okay. But it's not okay.'

Gillian is aware of the confusion between herself and Scully, and tries to clarify things as much as possible. She has appeared in several magazines in dramatically different clothes from Scully – she is clearly concerned that the two people are merging into one. There are, in fact, a whole host of differences between Gillian and Scully. Educational backgrounds vary enormously, and Gillian has her dubious punk background, something that Scully would never have dreamed of. Gillian is known on set for being a giggly actress, who frequently ruins takes by bursting into fits of laughter. In contrast, Scully has smiled only three times in four seasons, and laughed only once. On a lesser note, Gillian has a small tattoo on her ankle, and a birthmark above her upper lip, both of which are always covered up for shooting. Obviously they have similar mannerisms and Gillian does not put on a voice for the part, so they are both softly spoken, with the characteristic minimal movement of the mouth, like a ventriloquist. And they both appear to have no life outside of *The X-Files*. Otherwise they are distinctly different.

Perhaps the biggest difference of all is the fact that Gillian is actually a believer, whereas Scully is the hardened sceptic. Scully's scientific ideas are well-documented, but Gillian is almost the equivalent of Mulder, and she is quite open in the media about these ideas: 'I just always have had a fascination in paranormal-like subjects. I've always been fascinated by ESP and psychokinesis, and the whole subject of aliens and life on other planets. It's not something that I've sought out, I haven't gone out and read books on it, I just find it fascinating and so, because of that fascination, I've developed some sort of desire to believe in, or understanding of, that subject manner.

'I've had many experiences in my life – not paranormal experiences – as I'm sure many people have, where you think "God, that was a miracle that I just didn't get hit by that bus." Or when you say something at the same time as somebody else, three times in a row. It's fascinating – it makes you think. Or when somebody in your family is near death and they come back to life. It's life, it's fascinating stuff that happens all the time. [We should] pay attention to that stuff, and what I'm talking about is more on a spiritual than a paranormal level – I'm not talking about the evil stuff – just the things that we have to be grateful for in life. I think that this whole craze of aliens and angels and stuff is people reaching out there and wanting to feel better, and

The cerebral yet demure character of Scully has helped to break down many of the stereotypical and sexist portrayals of women in television.

for the pain to go away. In my mind, the odds that there is life on other planets is greater than there not being life on other planets. That's just in my head.'

She calls herself 'a fully fledged believer', keeps *The Tibetan Book of Living and Dying* with her at all times, and has also said, 'I'm not that much of a sceptic. I do believe in UFOs . . . on a certain level, I've just known or assumed it to be reality. In that respect [me and Scully] are very different.' This goes back to her honeymoon when she and Clyde were looking at the Hawaiian skies for UFOs. In the *Observer*, Gillian admitted to seeing psychics on several occasions, and held a lengthy conversation about this subject, which revealed much about her feelings on the subject, and how they differ drastically from Scully's: 'I have [seen psychics]. It is not a regular thing I do, but I have. They have been useful, but I can't give you examples. It is more guidance at a particular time. You don't ask specific questions of the Tarot cards . . . I believe there is a natural order to things, and that we are here to learn and to grow and to enrich our soul.

'All the information in the world is here with us and it's just a matter of tuning into it. The Tarot is a way to access that information.' When the interviewer turned and asked if everyone has a spirit guide, Gillian was equally forthcoming: 'I'm sure I do. Everybody does, one or many. But it is not something I think about too much, or something I preach.'

Her husband Clyde confirms this slant: 'Gillian is very spiritual, in search of whatever explanations might be out there.' Gillian also revealed how she is returning to the quasi-religion that she initially rejected as a child: 'When I was in high school, I was in a very atheist crowd and it was the consensus that religion was a crutch, but over the past few years I have grown to appreciate that feeling of safety or trust, that there is a light at the end of the tunnel and that there is a reason for us to be here.' At the same time, she says some of *The X-Files* scripts scare her so much that she 'freaks out', while others are so far-fetched she cannot relate to them at all. Despite this, she is more than happy to say, 'I'd like to see an alien very much. It wouldn't surprise me if there were a government cover-up. It seems so likely that there's something other than us in this universe. Cover-up is synonymous with government. It just is.' Mulder would be proud of her.

As if to confirm the differences between herself and Scully, Gillian is sure that if the two characters met in a bar they would have little to talk about (Gillian doesn't think she would even watch *The X-Files* regularly if she were not involved in it). Not that they wouldn't get on; she just feels that Scully, being 'insanely intelligent', would find the talk a little boring. 'Three-quarters of the information in her mind will never be in mine,' she told *BC Woman*, 'and she's fearless, I can't imagine going into some of the dark places she goes into. She's also quite close-minded. I act more on my intuition, and I'm more interested in the paranormal.' During a hiatus, Gillian admits to 'missing Scully, I love her and start getting excited when it's time to start filming the new series, because I want to be with her again'.

The problem for Gillian Anderson is that she worries about being typecast. The issue is not so much being *type*-cast as *Scully*-cast. People won't even accept her playing similar roles to Scully, let alone different roles. In the public's eye she is as much Special Agent Scully as she is Gillian Anderson, as much her character as Leonard Nimoy is Spock. The lack of exposure before this role means than, unlike Duchovny, she has no prior image to fall back on, no range of roles. Her own eagerness to behave 'as Scully might' in public appearances in order not to disappoint the viewers merely reinforces this dilemma. Gillian herself appears quite confident that this will not be a problem, as she told *SFX* magazine: 'The stuff that's being offered to me at the moment is a far cry from Scully. I haven't had any actual film offers yet, but there have been TV movies, although I haven't done any.'

She talks openly in the press of her desire to move into films when *The X-Files* is finished, and hints at the careers of people like Isabelle Adjani, Emma Thompson, Patricia Arquette, Ralph Fiennes and Gary Oldman as peer actors and actresses whom she aspires to. She has also talked of comedy, 'but only classy comedy, not the *Dumb and Dumber* kind'. She told *Movieline* magazine: 'I don't want to do a "Movie of the Week". I want a small role in a feature – that's my fantasy. The script would be what's important. I like movies that have something to say, or say nothing extremely well, like *Pulp Fiction*.' Also, on the subject of cinema: 'Films are my next big move, but I'm trying to be very careful about what I choose for my first role. I have a lot of favourite directors: Quentin Tarantino is one of them. I'd also like to work with Mike Leigh. Then there's Mike Nichols, and I think Ron Howard's a great film director . . . '

Unfortunately, the issue is not whether she will be offered roles – in her position she surely will. The issue is whether the public will accept her in these roles. Try Arnold Schwarzenegger in his comedy films, or Sylvester Stallone in *Stop! Or My Momma Will Shoot*, or how about Pamela Anderson in *King Lear*? Appearing in the forthcoming *X-Files* movie will only serve to reinforce this dilemma, as then she will be known on the large screen as well as the small screen as Scully. True, Gillian is financially stable for life, but creatively she is already at a dead end. She is known throughout sixty countries and by forty million people as Agent Scully, and that will take some changing.

THE CHURCH OF THE IMMACULATE GILLIAN

Our Philosophy:

1. We believe that Gillian Anderson is a Goddess.
2. Clyde Klotz, Gillian's husband, is 'The Chosen One' (or 'That Lucky Bastard' – worshipper's choice).
3. Gillian's daughter, Piper, is considered to be 'The Next Goddess'.
   This is the holy trinity of the Church of the Immaculate Gillian.
   All members will respect this holy trinity.

During the Cold War the military were very concerned that, in the event of a nuclear blast, high-level communications between the underground bunkers of leading figures would be destroyed. Power lines would be lost, buildings destroyed and so on. As a result, vast sums of money and pools of researchers were assigned to develop a method whereby communications could be kept open in the event of such a crisis. The system they came up with was a computer-based network that allowed digital information to be relayed at great speed, with security and clarity. In the event, the Cold War evaporated into the relative warmth of glasnost and perestroika, and the system was never actually needed for this purpose.

However, by this time, various educational institutions had come across the idea and found that it was perfect for many of their own communication systems. From the germ of an idea, the system flourished and by the mid-to late-eighties was blossoming into a web of computers that were all joined across the globe. The Internet had arrived.

By 1991, the Net was beginning to go public, with the media and general public fast being drawn to the information superhighway, or as some called it, cyberspace. Commercial enterprises recognised the vast financial potential in presenting their products to millions of users on-line. Pretty soon, there were millions of sites covering a colossal array of subjects: films, television, music, media, health, environment, history, pleasure – you name it, the Net covered it.

A community was developing around the system, which had its own language, its own ethics and mutual interests that knitted them together. Many of the early users were students, who were both computer-literate and had access to an e-mail address and the so-called worldwide web via their own university or college system server. By the mid-nineties, it was clear that the Net was in fact very much more than a faddy piece of futuristic software, and that it was here to stay.

The relationship between *The X-Files* and the Internet is perhaps unique. Never before has a show had such an intimate relationship with the system – and central to that rapport is Gillian Anderson/Dana Scully. There is a strong argument that most Internet users are predominantly 16- to 35-year-old males, with an interest in computers and/or predisposition to technological advances. Ironically, this is the same group who are frequently fascinated by science fiction, and so it is a regular occurrence that a Net user is also a fan of programmes like *Star Wars*, *Star Trek*, cult films such as *Dazed and Confused* and, of course, *The X-Files*.

What is fascinating about the Net and *The X-Files* is that in many senses the Net discovered the programme before the media did. From the start, *The X-Files* lit up the fibre optic channels running across the world with discussions about that week's episode, the characters, the story-lines and so on. As the series increased in popularity the Net became swamped with sites and information about it. At the present moment, *The X-Files*' presence on the Internet is nothing short of breathtaking. Hundreds of sites are dedicated to *The X-Files* alone, with forty specifically for David Duchovny and over eighty for Gillian Anderson. *The X-Files* is referenced on a further eight thousand sites. Second only to *Star Trek*, it is the major Internet television show.

The success of the Net has coincided with the success of *The X-Files* and thus created a peculiar new beast – *The X-Files* fanatic, or the so-called X Phile. No self-respecting X Phile ignores the Internet presence. Indeed, many will spend hours talking about their favourite show, highlighting mistakes in the set detail (so-called 'Net Picking') and offering solutions, or ideas for plots. In time, this environment has created a very odd type of fanaticism, and none more so than with Gillian Anderson. The most noted fan clubs are The Genuine Admirers of Gillian Anderson (GAGA) and The Gillian Anderson Testosterone Brigade (GATB). Her fan clubs call her IDDD or 'Intellectually Drop Dead Gorgeous' – this became the subject of a semantic debate, after which some admirers changed the phrase to 'Gorgeously Drop-Dead Intellectual', which they felt was 'a tad less randy'. There is even an Israeli fan club page! The GAGA admit they are indeed 'gaga'

Gillian's 'specs-appeal' has attracted hordes of admirers.

over the actress. There is the Society For The Prevention Of Cruelty To Gillian Anderson and even The Queeuqeq Memorial Small Yappy Dog Rest Home, in memory of Scully's recently deceased dog (named, they will all tell you, after another character in *Moby Dick*). One fan even asked about a 'One Night Stand Scully' action figure, complete with standard business suit – 'Think of the packaging!' he said.

Admiration for Gillian (and indeed the programme) is evident in more than just the fan club sites. The Internet newsgroups are awash with references to the show, and it even has its own newsgroup, entitled 'alt.tv. x-files'. Swap shops and sales of *X-Files* merchandise and rarities cram these pages – one fan bought Scully's plastic FBI pass laminate for $1500. The Net is never more busy than immediately after a new episode – in Season Four, when Mulder casually announced that Scully had 'a date', the Internet lit up with frantic Gillian fans desperate for more talk. Indeed, the Net had been busy discussing this option ever since someone leaked the script a few weeks previously. She's a Catholic, some of them said. She would never date, it would take away from her job, criticised others. Chris Carter is losing sight of her character, came another claim. Who would she date? When? Where? These and many more questions cram onto the Internet newsgroups daily.

Chris Carter and his team have been acutely aware of this since the show began, and, being fans of the Net themselves, they have developed a unique bond between these Netters and themselves, such that *The X-Files* has become perhaps the world's first truly interactive television show – the Internet has become an integral part of *The X-Files* experience. Carter and colleagues (including Gillian) regularly go on-line and chat to viewers, discuss where the show is failing, or what might be interesting to see, or how they have reacted to events so far. The electronic sigh of relief when Scully returned after her abduction was audible across the whole network.

Carter himself is very keen to see this continue, as he told *Sci-Fi Buzz* magazine: 'It puts pressure on us to keep us honest. We've got to be honest in our science, our research has to be accurate because we've got a big science-based audience out there who watches us very carefully and loves to "pick our nits", and so that keeps us honest. I think we have to please that audience to maintain our popularity.' The one error he made was in trying to christen them the dreadfully clumsy File-O-Philes, a moniker which was soon replaced by X Phile.

Concerns that the show will become too self-referential are, possibly, too harsh; it is refreshing to see a successful show prepared to speak directly to its audience, and take feedback and constructive criticism so openly. Although neither Gillian Anderson nor David Duchovny is an Internet enthusiast, they are both aware of the ongoing presence. Duchovny once logged on to find fans discussing why Scully never adjusts the car seat after the much taller Mulder has been driving: 'That was probably the last time I ever looked at the Internet, because that kind of frightened me, I didn't want to see myself scrutinised in such a fashion.'

Gillian is a little more charitable (she has considerably more sites dedicated to her): 'I think it's wonderful, I mean, it has been helping the show and it's wonderful that we have a constant following. I haven't actually logged on myself, but I'm aware of their presence.' She later told *Starlog*: 'Just recently I saw some stuff for the first time. It's pretty amazing how involved it gets. I see myself, if I really got involved, spending hours reading stuff, but my energy needs to be in other areas right now.' She is also wary of what she reads affecting her acting: 'That's one reason I don't participate, because it's very personal stuff, and in terms of the character I don't want to be influenced too much by people's opinions. I have to stick very closely as to how I feel how the character needs to be portrayed from episode to episode.' She also said: 'It is something that's taking place in a very different reality than one that I'm living in.'

Nevertheless, Gillian has gone on-line for IRC chats on several occasions, whereby people can log on and ask questions direct to the star. On such occasions the lines have been flooded, barely able to cope with the response. Usually the fans keep their questions respectable, but occasionally the weirder X Philes rear up. Take, for example, this question posed to Gillian: 'What public figures does Gillian Anderson think she'd like an affair with? Are they available and can we film this?' (There is also a rumour that Scully's bras have to be kept on the top shelf and behind locked doors in the wardrobe room on set, for fear of fans trying to capture such a prize).

X Philes are perhaps similar to Trekkies, though a difference is that with Trekkies the vast majority only came out of the woodwork after the show had been cancelled. X Philes, by contrast, have been there from its very inception, and have even contributed to its evolution. The crew even play games with the massed Net audience now, by placing red herrings in the script details for them to spot and even going so far as to snub them in the show – in one episode Mulder is invited back to 'netpick' with some trainspotter types, but he politely, although firmly declines, saying he has to go home and do his laundry. This is a more polite echo of the infamous snub by William Shatner when he said that obsessed Trekkies should 'get a life'.

A large number of X Philes have a distinct fascination with Gillian Anderson, such that it is almost a prerequisite to feel this way. The Internet is preoccupied with discussions about whether she is sexy, intellectual, tarty, and so on. This is why Gillian, ever-mindful of not wanting to be seen simply as Scully, decided to shoot all those provocative photo sessions in 1995 and 1996. Even though she knew she had a big following, she was shocked by the response to these pictures. The most famous of these was a sexy photo shoot she did for the April 1995 issue of *FHM* in Britain, a magazine which called her 'The World's Sexiest Woman'. With a seductive Gillian lounging, scantily clad, on a bed, the issue was the magazine's best-ever seller, and now pristine copies are highly sought after. The *FHM* office once received a signed cheque for $200 from one desperate fan. She also appeared in *New Woman* in a tight-fitting rubber catsuit, and has frequently been photographed in skimpy knickers or even less!

X-File newsgroups still resound with Wanted Ads asking for these photos. Similarly popular was the Australian edition of *Rolling Stone* magazine, which pictured a seemingly naked Anderson and Duchovny in bed, apparently post-coital. The issue sparked all sorts of rumours about on and off-set activity. Needless to say, it was done as a piece of fun, knowing it would cause a furore. On unofficial Internet sites, admiration of Gillian is taken one step further by fans faking pornographic pictures of her, transposing her face onto glamour models' naked bodies. Back in the real world, she was even offered a centrespread and front cover feature in *Playboy*, for, it is claimed, hundreds of thousands of dollars, but she is reported to have turned it down without hesitation.

Whilst many fans welcome this distraction (at least the male ones do anyway), some are more reserved and protective. One girl at a shopping mall appearance said, 'There have been some instances when part of your brassiere has been shown, and so how can we respect you?' She was resoundly booed for her cheek. Another Net user put it rather more convolutedly: 'Let me insert a caveat. I am not interested in passing judgement about the transitions in persona which I perceive in images of Gillian Anderson. I am in no way nostalgic for the "pure" visions which were more consonant with the character of Scully. My only point is to note the transition and perhaps speculate on it for its implications for society in general.' Yes, okay.

Gillian herself is amazed by the claims of being the 'sexiest woman in the world', and frankly seems to find it all rather hilarious, as she told *FHM* magazine: 'I don't particularly feel like a sex symbol, but then somebody asked me the other day what it was like to work with a sex god like David Duchovny, and I can't get that out of my head. Sex god?' Despite what her modesty denies, she is very much a sex symbol – when *TV Guide* in America criticised her hairstyle, the angry response by hundreds of Gillian fans shocked even that hardened tabloid publication. She also said, 'I've been called "an unconventional beauty" which is a strange kind of compliment, but I know I'm not a marketable beauty in TV terms. I'm attractive in a different kind of way.'

Gillian's popularity particularly rocketed during Season Three, to the extent that by the start of 1996 she was perhaps the main star of the show. This is reflected in two very frantic public appearances she made around that time. Firstly at *The X-Files* Convention at Burbank, and then at various Australian shopping-mall appearances on a promotional tour. The former

Gillian signing X-Files *merchandise at* The X-Files *Convention at Burbank Hilton Hotel.*

was an official gathering at the Burbank Airport Hilton Convention Center, in the standing-room only ballroom with a capacity for 1500 people. The hall was packed with stalls of merchandise and related *X-Files* paraphernalia, all official of course, and despite the $35-$50 daily entry fees the hall was busy. Saturday was not sold out (only about six hundred in attendance), but on the Sunday, with an abundance of press passes swamping the hall, the venue was crammed full (one disgruntled X Phile spotted a young lady handing out three free press passes to her very young children).

Since Duchovny was not in attendance at the Burbank event, the expectation for Gillian was enormous. Before she appeared twelve minutes of footage from the show was played, with huge cheers going up after each clip, the biggest roar being reserved for the last snippet, when everyone knew what was next. Then on she came, up onto the stage to a roar of applause and a blinding barrage of flash bulbs from the massed ranks of the paparazzi and hundreds of fans. Her reaction was immediate and revealing: 'Holy cow! I have no idea what to say right now! It's unbelievable. I'm completely *verklempt.*'

Clearly shaken by the audience's reaction to her, Gillian composed herself and said: 'You know, I wanted to prepare about ten or fifteen minutes of something extremely witty and charming, and honestly, if I had, I wouldn't remember it right now.' Instead, she opened up the floor to all questions and was obviously not short of takers. Afterwards, she still seemed to be in shell shock – perhaps this was the first direct sign of just how much adoration she had attracted: 'I was very nervous going in, I wasn't sure what to expect and, and I came out feeling much less nervous about it. The audience was wonderful, they were terrific, they were all very sane – most of them were – very sane and just very sweet and wonderful and they were just there because they love the show and it ended up being a wonderful experience.'

The second indication of the blossoming Gillian Anderson phenomenon came on her tour of Australia in the summer of 1996. As not many celebrities make the trip 'Down Under', when they do the turn-out is usually large. Gillian was due first at the Southland Shopping Mall. Prior to this event, her only such appearance had been at a small bookshop in Munich. Understandably, Gillian was extremely startled when she was told there were over twelve thousand people waiting outside to greet her.

The day soon turned into high drama when the sheer numbers started to cause a crush. As Gillian walked on stage there was a rush towards her, and in the melée many people were hurt. Even with extra police and security staff on duty crowd control was difficult. The organisers had to appeal for calm over the PA system as fans fainted everywhere – within minutes the ambulances on

Gillian has had to become used to the trappings of stardom,
including the endless signing of autographs.

stand-by had been filled with over twenty hyperventilating teenagers and people with minor crush injuries. Gillian was terrified, and had to take the microphone herself to appeal for calm: 'People are getting squashed. We don't want to have to do any autopsies.' The situation deteriorated as injured youngsters had to be pulled from the seething pit of bodies.

When calm was finally restored, Gillian answered hordes of questions from the fans. Meanwhile, several startling facts had emerged from the chaos which indicated the near-worship that centred around Gillian. The first in the queue to get her autograph was a man who had slept in the shopping centre car-park and started to queue at 2 a.m. Many of the teenagers who fainted had been queueing since 8 a.m. without food or water, and in the words of one ambulance man, 'Their breathing-rate changed when the lady from *The X-Files* came on stage.' One woman was carried away on a stretcher, unconscious, clutching a still-unsigned video. Meanwhile, a man who put his bags down to help the injured had them stolen, with over $1000-worth of shopping taken. Another fan who lost out was a gentleman whose $80 jacket was stolen, but he said he would go home happy as he managed to get her autograph on two items of merchandise. In the end, the appearance had to be shut down half an hour early to prevent serious injury to the hysterical fans.

The next day, in the sanctuary of her hotel room, Gillian spoke to the *Melbourne Herald Sun* about the surreal episode: 'I've not experienced anything like it, I've never made a mall appearance before, so I really had no point of reference. The welcome here has been overwhelming – absolutely incredible. It has taken some coming to terms with.' She went on to say, 'I could definitely only do this kind of thing [promotional tours] once a year for short periods.'

The tour was so busy she barely had time to sight-see in Australia, although she did go snorkelling with some grey sharks in the tank at Manly's Ocean World. There was precious little time for anything else, however, and the same scenes of hysteria were repeated on each of the three city stops she made while promoting *The X-Files* video – over 30,000 people queued to see her in just three dates. At the second appearance, over eighty people were pulled from the crowd. At the front of this crowd a thirteen-year-old girl was spotted with the word 'Scully' painted across her forehead, and an 'X' on each cheek – this Scully fan had been there since 5 a.m. First in the autograph queue this time was a thirty-something father of two, Peter Brown, who said with an almost teenybopperish joy: 'It's the best show. Scully's gorgeous, I'm thrilled, thrilled, I can't wait.'

Despite these scenes of total fanaticism, Gillian seemed to be in denial about her shooting star. At the first Golden Globe awards, she seemed genuinely shocked that the programme had won. She was typically gracious when Duchovny wasn't nominated for an Emmy as she had been, though he was reported to have described it as 'a confusing omission'. In Australia, upon her arrival at Sydney International Airport she appeared bemused that the walls of photographers were there to capture her on film: 'I'd go insane. If I honestly allowed myself to believe that twelve thousand people would show up to see me, then I'd be somebody I'm not.' It was clearly a situation she was not comfortable with, as she told Sydney's *Sunday Telegraph*: 'I tend to be very private, so I don't get off on the paparazzi following you around, or the intrusion aspect of it. Or being in places where there are lots of people. I don't like big crowds. If you're in a vulnerable state of mind in any way, it can be incredibly intrusive and disorientating to place yourself in a situation where there are hundreds of people who want your attention and want you to live up to their standards. It gets emotionally exhausting.'

Gillian receives some sisterly advice from veteran star, Lauren Bacall at the premiere of If These Walls Could Talk.

THE EX FILES FOR DIVORCE

Mulder: 'Do you believe in the after-life, Scully?'
Scully: 'I'd settle for a life in this one.'

By late 1996 *The X-Files* and its two key actors were household names. In particular, Gillian Anderson had seen the year out as the newly-crowned sexiest woman in the world, and had taken over from Duchovny in terms of awards, high-profile chat shows and magazine front covers. Rumours that their relationship was frosty were still rife, and now that she was perhaps more famous than he, these increased. Duchovny, meanwhile, had remained his dry and reserved self. Their infamously long working days remained, and the intense pressures on everyone involved with the series were mounting with every new accolade.

Gillian had come through her pregnancy with admirable resilience, but now the stakes were much higher. Her privacy had long been lost, she was unable to walk down the streets of Vancouver anonymously any longer, and her protection of her daughter and husband from the world's peering media gave their home a feeling of a prison. The costs of her fame and money were starting to become painfully apparent.

Initially, Gillian had been very positive about her role and the beneficial effect it had had on her life. Now she hinted at her changed attitude in interviews, although, as ever, she was far from forthcoming: 'Well, yeah. There are times when I wish that it would stop, but I wish that something would happen and I wouldn't have to work sixteen hours back-to-back anymore. Then I have a good day and the work is good and the script is good and it's a pleasure, and everything goes smoothly and I change my mind. It's just like life, you know?'

She also said to the *Herald Sun TV Guide*: 'All of us are going to remember it and feel like it was some of the best years of our lives, we've really bent the rules – taken a lot of risks. We've been a part of something special, and there is a real feeling of pride in being involved in something like this and having it succeed . . . mind you, when *X-Files* finishes I will never do another TV series.'

These feelings of discontent reared their heads most publicly in a piece in the *Los Angeles Times* when Gillian was quoted as saying that working to the show's schedule was like 'a death sentence'. Regulars on set were dismayed, and Chris Carter felt betrayed – after all, it was he who had championed her right from the word go; he had taken her on despite her lack of experience. What was more, she was not the only one – all her colleagues were working these ridiculously long hours too. 'I was upset,' Carter acknowledges. 'I called her and said, "Look, this is a chance of a lifetime. The work is so hard, I'm sure it feels as if you've signed your life away. But if we all felt like that, we might as well go home and pack it up."'

Gillian apologised to him and the rest of the crew, but it was a sign of things to come. There were rumours that she was becoming enveloped in her own star status, throwing tantrums, acting like a prima donna. She was apparently engrossed in the dilemma of who was the best designer for Scully – was it Fiso Verani, Jax, Armani or Maximara? She was alleged to hardly ever sign autographs, dismissing the signature hunters with little grace, and it was said to be months since she had bothered to read any of her (admittedly large) amounts of fan mail. This was all in stark contrast to her earlier attitude, when she had been famous for her humility and normality on set. Now she had a hairdresser, personal assistants, nannies, and a designer wardrobe crammed with expensive clothes. Gillian had certainly taken on many of the external trappings of celebrity, as this 'LA/Hollywood-speak' quote shows: 'I'm not in the right head-space to deal with intrusion, even if it's wonderful people saying they like the show. I try to be gracious but at times I draw the line. Have I remained sane? You have to accept the price.'

Clearly she was beginning to yearn for a release from the rigours of being Scully, which could not possibly fit in with a married family life. She was getting more and more vocal about her restlessness, as she told the *Radio Times*: 'I was a little restless after the first year and felt I was stuck in this situation. Now I try to focus on the fact that it's only a small period of time in a long life. It will be over before we know it, and it's done for most of us what nothing else could have. I don't know about being set up for life financially, but it will help tremendously in terms of careers.' More worryingly, when she was asked if the job and her fame caused problems with Clyde, her husband, she said: 'There's no reason why it should, but it does, so let's not talk about it.'

Gillian has become a fully fledged sex symbol,
and numerous sexy photo shoots have done nothing to
harm her reputation.

WHO BLAIRS WINS! ELECTION REACTION SPECIAL

Melody Maker
May 17, 1997 85p

EVERYTHING MUST GO!
MANICS, SPACE and THE BEAUTIFUL SOUTH
at the Hillsborough Justice Concert

I SHOULD POGO!
SUPERGRASS, PLACEBO,
BECK and THE PRODIGY
live spectacular!

**COP AN EIFFEL
OF THIS!**
Down and out in Paris
with NICK CAVE

X and drugs

GILL
ANDE
Stealing, Scully, Sex W
The

KENICKIE ★ 3 COLOURS RED ★ EEL
TEENAGE FANCLUB ★ CAKE ★ ROL
JON SPENCER AND THE 'SEXMUSIK'

DAVID BOWIE! PAVEMENT! SILVERCHAIR!

Rolling Sto
The
X
ILES!

AN
ON

PHISH
'AMERICA'S
BIGGEST
JAM BAND!

COMAG £3.00

DISASTER ON EVEREST – A SURVIVOR'S STORY
Esquire
DECEMBER 1996/JANUARY 1997 £2.70

GILLIAN
ANDERSON
THE SECRET OF X APPEAL

PLUS OUR
FAVOURITE
WOMEN OF
THE YEAR

THE MAN WHO
MADE OASIS
'I nearly died from
drugs and booze'

WOULD
YOU FALL
FOR A THAI
BAR GIRL?
One man did
and liv
regret

SO YOU
THINK YOU
KNOW ABOUT
SPORT?
Test your
knowledge in
the ultimate
quiz

LOUISE
WENER
Sleeper's
sex symbol
mouths off

ER DOUGAL DEMI MOORE OASIS LIVE FRIENDS

KY
AZINE

FREE LAGER!
A CAN
OF XXXX
FOR EVERY
READER

Work? Sod
that...
SKY'S
COLLEGE
SPECIAL
•15 ways
to pull
a fresher
•Students
on the
game
•Sleeping
with
the landlady

"I used to be a good little girl"

GENT
SCULLY

and a secret past:
the real Gillian Anderson

DON'T WATCH JUST AN
the BOX
JUNE/JULY 1997 £1.95

Cr
Badgers

THE
NEARLY NEW
TELEVISION
MAGAZINE

X-FILES
INTERVIEW
DAVID
DUCHOVN

It's a
dirty job
but someone's
got to do it

FREE INSIDE: A H
SKI
THE FACT AND FICTION OF THE UNEXPLAINED

X
POSÉ

REBIRTH
Reincarnation:
the evidence

Series creator Chris Carter on the future of

THE X-FILES

DYLAN
and 49 other
terribly cool
televisual
dudes

101

It was interviews and quotes like these that led to strong rumours that Gillian had had enough and was leaving the show. However, she strongly denies this and was happy to put the record straight in the *Sunday Telegraph's TV Extra* magazine: 'I have promised Chris Carter that I would stay with the project, I'm hoping it will go as long as it needs to go. That we don't over-extend our welcome.'

Gillian had taken the role of Scully when she was 24. She was now a 28-year-old mother, and had had only one major role in her career. Whilst other actresses were broadening their range all the time, Gillian was becoming more and more typecast in that one role. She has done a few parts outside *The X-Files*: she did the voice of a character called EVE on Microsoft's game 'Hellbender'; she hosted Fox's *Why Planes Go Down* (a mystery-based show); she has done *The Simpsons* (with Duchovny, as two FBI agents who come to investigate Bart's apparent UFO sighting); she did a promo for *America's Most Wanted* and a series called *Spies Above*; and she has done the voices for a number of *X-Files* audio novels. So even in these other roles she seems inextricably tied up with the series. She knows this, and obviously wonders sometimes if she has done the right thing: 'In terms of steady work, it's brilliant, but sometimes you can't help but feel that wonderful parts are passing you by. I guess there's no point in wasting energy thinking about not having been able to do *Sense and Sensibility*, or whatever.'

It was obviously with this in mind that Gillian took more active steps to curtail this artistic restriction on her career. In early 1997, her film career started to take off. Although fans who were unaware of her earlier outing in *The Turning* talked of her 'debut movie', this was, in effect, her first major step into high profile, big screen productions. Furthermore, she decided to take two roles, not one, at the same time. First came the independent film *Hellcab*, which is set to star John Cusack, Laurie Metcalf and Julianne Moore.

More notably she also won a role in the big budget *Freak the Mighty*, with Sharon Stone as the star and executive producer, alongside Harry Dean Stanton and Gena Rowlands. The script, based on the Rodman Philbrick novel, is about a genius child who suffers from a degenerative disease and stops growing at the age of six, a chilling echo of Gillian's brother's childhood difficulties. Sharon Stone is his mother, and Gillian will be the white-trash character named Loretta, a strong start in her campaign against typecasting.

Summer 1997, meanwhile, sees the start of work on the big screen version of *The X-Files* before filming for the fifth (and some say last) season of the show starts in the autumn.

Gillian even found time to do the voice-over for UK-based techno band Hal's single. She first heard the music when it was used as a backing track on

Future Fantastic, asked the producer about it and was duly offered the chance to appear on her debut single. She told *Rolling Stone*'s David Lipsky in February 1997: '[I was] presented with some samples of stuff I could say, and it was quite poetic and erotic, and we came up with what I think is a really great dance single. It's hot. It's not a new career move by any means, but it made me feel fun and alive.' Already, then, Gillian is looking to expand her career horizons; whatever else is unsure in her future, there will be no shortage of work.

No doubt insiders had seen it coming, but to the outside world it was a huge shock when, on 13 January 1997, the tabloid headlines screamed: 'Ex Files For Divorce'. Several 'exclusive' stories all revealed the same thing: in October 1996 Gillian had left the family home she shared with Piper and Clyde, after falling for a bit-part actor who had appeared in some of *The X-Files* episodes. Rumour had it that she had already filed for divorce. Needless to say, the world's media descended on her house, on *The X-Files* production set, and on just about anyone who had ever been involved with the actress. Signs of the break-up had been there earlier on, when she told *Sky* magazine: 'Anybody in the situation I'm in right now would be hard to be married to. I'm strong-willed. I want to do what I want to do. I'm not controlling, but I know what I want.' In 1996 she had also said: 'I am more ambitious than my husband. I have things to accomplish. I will do what I need to move forward to wherever is my destiny.'

What made matters worse was that the media quickly painted her as the villain, allegedly leaving a loving husband and charming young daughter to run off with a toy-boy she had only recently met. Clyde was left entrenched in his home to face the press, but said only that 'any talk of a divorce is premature'. That week he quit their £1.4 million mansion and moved into a shabby, £100-per-week flat in downtown Vancouver, where he was said to be looking after Piper. However, the paparazzi would not let him rest there either, with unsubstantiated reports of a 'old flame' brunette leaving the house after hours of heart-to-hearts.

Gillian, meanwhile, was said to be 'coy and giggly' about her new lover, and seemingly rather disparaging about Clyde: 'My husband bores me . . . the marriage is over and I have outgrown him.' The *Sun* reported an insider as saying, 'Clyde is gutted. He is desperate for a reconciliation, but Gillian says she's outgrown him. Her career has just rocketed and she's become the most lusted-after woman in the world. She just feels they've got nothing in common apart from their daughter. Gillian has been complaining she feels stifled in the marriage.'

Intrusion into Gillian's private life increased as
rumours of marital breakdown hit the headlines.

hasked: The Briton
an dumped her X for

MONSTER ROLE: Adrian Hughes in TV make-up

'Adrian swore
his family
to secrecy
and his
mother was
terrified
that the
truth would
get out'

EXCLUSIVE
BY JOHN CHAPMAN

ALIENATED: Gillian and her husband

THE EX FIL

Scully falls for toyboy
extra on hit TV show

OLD FLAME: Gill hugs hubby Clyde

AT HOME: Her Vancouver mansion

STAYING MUM: With daughter Piper

Private

Ambitious

WORLD'S
100 MOST
Beautiful
WOMEN
The top
12
GILLIAN
ANDERSON

MIRROR, Mirror on the wall, with
Soccer Sausage you'll have a ball

X-FILES
SCULLY
DITCHES
HUSBAND

Mirror EXCLUSIVE: The truth is.. she's got a toyboy

SEE
PAGE 3

It was rumoured that the calm, dependable and loyal characteristics of Clyde had become boring to the star actress, who in the time she had known him had rocketed from unknown actress to the one of world's top TV stars. The very things that attracted her to him in the first place were now splitting them apart. The same insider said, 'Gillian's become this massive star but Clyde hasn't changed. He still hangs out with the same friends, he goes to the same favourite restaurant almost every night . . . and he hates it when people call him Mr Gillian Anderson.'

Gillian had not been seen over Christmas 1996 and the New Year. Then it emerged that she had in fact visited her new boyfriend's family, which was in the decidedly unglamorous Walking, in East Yorkshire. Here she strolled around largely unnoticed, in a thick winter coat to shield her from the biting cold and snow. Her lover was called Adrian Hughes, although his family carried the name Hockey. He was either 32 or 23, depending on the source (and hence either a toy-boy or a sugar daddy) and was the proud owner of 1997's most talked about goatee beard.

The press inevitably tracked Gillian down to Walking – however, Adrian's mother claimed she had never heard of the man and that their family had nothing to do with the scandal. In a rather odd interview given on the doorstep she said, 'It's rubbish. My son's called Sam and he lives in New Mexico and I haven't seen him for years. My daughter Pippa visited Canada and interviewed Gillian Anderson last year, that's the only connection the family has with *The X-Files*.' The newspapers suggested all the secrecy was to avoid any negative effect on a possible forthcoming custody case over Piper.

Apparently, Adrian had left Britain for Canada in his youth, when his parents' own marriage had ended in divorce, and had followed his father to the new country. While there he began acting, and in the course of many auditions landed a small role in *The X-Files*. It was, seemingly, on set that he and Gillian fell for each other. Rumour had it that he was by Gillian's side in London that New Year's week when she recorded the voice-over for a pop single. All this time, Piper was in Canada with her father. By Canadian law, Clyde stands to get half the earnings she made whilst married to him – estimated to be in the region of £3 million. It was now also revealed that he had probably been sacked, rather than resigned, from *The X-Files* after Gillian had become pregnant.

The night this 'scandalous' news was announced, *The X-Files* newsgroup on the Internet was ablaze with discussion. Within minutes there was a discussion group entitled 'Scully – Saint or Slut?': two opposing camps sided against one another over whether Clyde was a wimp or whether Gillian was a careerist prima donna. Many hundreds of besotted Gillian fans now revelled in the fact that their idol was single again (almost). Others, perhaps a tad more realistic, just ruminated on the negative effect this would have on young Piper, and how the couple had probably married much too soon after first meeting each other. One fan posted, speculatively, 'Ten Reasons That Gillian Dumped Her Husband'. The more weird ones noted that there was a paranormal coincidence in that Gillian had a new love in her life the same month that Season Four's much-debated 'date' for Scully was broadcast.

Within three weeks things had taken another, much darker turn. Again the tabloids splashed the news first. Gillian's alleged new boyfriend had, it was reported, been arrested and charged with five serious sexual assaults over a four-year period, on three different women. In effect, he stands accused of being a serial sex attacker. In total, five women accuse him of sexual assault, and a further two of rape. All the women are in their twenties, and claim to have come forward to stop him attacking future victims. All the charges were laid long before his relationship with Gillian was thought to have begun, and none of them knew about the other attacks.

One of the alleged victims is *X-Files* production assistant Lavonne Rathie, who claims she was raped and beaten senseless by Hughes in November 1991. She had a court order banning Hughes from approaching her, but that had to be eased to allow Hughes to have 'professional contact' with her at work. He was apparently charged with her rape five years previously but these charges were later dropped due to unexplained 'technicalities'. Several of the other women have court restraining orders banning him from approaching them. One victim was quoted as saying, 'Hughes is a beast . . . it's only fun for him if it's forced.' One alleged victim said Hughes invited her in to watch *The Little Mermaid*: 'Before I knew it, I was on the floor and he was touching my private parts.'

The alleged attacker was also said to be known around Vancouver bars as a yob, and has been banned from two drinking establishments, with a court appearance set to answer these charges. Hughes has apparently confirmed the charges, but has otherwise been dodging the tabloid frenzy that inevitably surrounded him and his supposed relationship with Gillian. There is no evidence, of course, to suggest that Gillian has been attacked.

Meanwhile, the siege of Hughes' family in Yorkshire intensified. Under mounting pressure from the press, his mother changed her story and now claimed, 'They have worked together, are in the same social circle and are close friends.' Court documents show that his real name is Stanley Adrian Hockey. He denies any affair with Gillian, saying that the relationship is purely platonic, and that Gillian and his sister Pippa are good friends. As for the supposed, cosy New Year holiday, it is claimed she stayed with his family as a

friend whilst recording this unknown pop promo, and that she washed dishes, played games, and had a snowball fight in the garden – nothing more. It emerged that Hughes played one of the brothers in what was arguably *The X-Files'* most gruesome episode, Season Four's 'Home', although one hopes for Gillian's sake that he looks a little better than the severely deformed Sherman Nathaniel Peacock.

After the initial furore over her marriage break-up, Gillian commented: 'There's nothing in these love stories. Our relationship is purely platonic and nothing more. We have become good friends, and obviously get on. But it's just ludicrous the way people figure we're an item.' After the news of the sex charges broke, the rumours came, swiftly, that Gillian had finished with Hughes. First, apparently, she wasn't seeing him and now she had dumped him. There was said to be grave concern in the Anderson camp about the negative affects this terrible publicity would have on the actress's court case for custody of her daughter Piper – during all this, Clyde had been described as a stable and caring father. Unfortunately this bad press was unavoidable, and her name was now inextricably linked to Hughes.

When the media tracked him down to his home in Kitsilano near Vancouver, Hughes said: 'It's just hell, and I'm sick and tired of it. It's got to the point where I've run out and intimidated a couple of British tabloid reporters in front of my house. My home is under siege, my mom's home in England is under siege, my agency is under siege, my friends' homes are under siege, my friends' friends' homes are under siege. As far as anything I discuss with Ms Anderson, it's not up for comment.' He went on: 'First of all, I have a girlfriend, and her name is not Gillian. And, number two, Gillian Anderson and I are friends. And my relationship with my girlfriend and my relationship with Gillian may be coming to an end because of all this.'

As if this wasn't enough, there were serious rumblings of trouble at *The X-Files* set. Firstly, Duchovny was reported as saying he wasn't sure he could carry on after Season Five. He talked in *Rolling Stone* of the programme being a burden, of his fears of typecasting and that he would be 'relieved when the show is over'. He predicted difficulties would soon arise if the two leading actors were not careful: 'What is odious is your life becoming public. Once you lose your anonymity, you don't realise what a great loss that is until it's gone and then you can never get it back. Even if your career spirals downward, you can never get your anonymity back. You go from being a hero to being a joke and neither is very pleasant.'

Chris Carter reportedly suggested that he, too, was thinking of 'bailing out' – he said he would only stay on for further seasons 'when they start rolling in the Seinfeld money' ($1 million per episode). Then Gillian was

Rumour became fact when the new man in Gillian's life escorted her to the Screen Actors Guild Awards *in February 1997.*

alleged to have filed a lawsuit, and stated that she would refuse to sign up for the forthcoming *X-Files* movie unless her wages were put on a level with Duchovny's – they still lagged behind, despite her earlier protests. All this came at the start of Season Four which, ironically, drew higher ratings than any other season opener in the show's history. But worse was to come. The rumours started that Scully had cancer and was to be written out of the show.

This all started in when Scully's nose started bleeding strangely in 'Leonard Betts'. All sorts of Internet rumours flew about the repercussions of this, but the word on the inside was that she had a tumour. Was it related to the alien implant found in the back of her neck after she had been abducted? Or was it a warning shot from the show's producers that more wage increases could cost Gillian her job? X Philes panicked, saying, how could they kill her off when the character Clyde Bruckman had said she would not die? Who would watch the programme if she left? It seems highly unlikely that she will be killed off, but with *The X-Files*, you never know . . .

To throw some more confusion into the pot, there were even rumours that Gillian and Duchovny were actually dating. Highly scurrilous and utterly unsubstantiated, they stemmed from a kiss Duchovny planted near to Gillian's mouth at the successful 1997 Golden Globe Awards, where both of them had won an award alongside the Best Drama award for the show. There was talk of the two of them being seen socialising around Vancouver, which had never happened before. She was single, Duchovny had had a difficult year for girlfriends – why not?

The Golden Globe success should have been a time for celebration. Unfortunately, with the whole environment in such turmoil it was only the cause of yet more speculation. Gillian's Armani dress sense was derided by many, but more worryingly some observers noted that she appeared very drunk at the ceremony, staggering around with a glazed expression. She neglected to thank Duchovny when she accepted her award with a boring and dull speech, and appeared ill at ease the whole night. People hinted at the return of her alleged past problems with alcohol. The Internet went into a frenzy with such severe discussion as 'Die Scully Die!!' and 'Gillian Anderson – the Whore of Grand Rapids'.

Whatever the outcome of Gillian's complicated love life and this whole sordid mess, her celebrity status means that she will always be in the spotlight. Hopefully, she will progress to bigger and better things, but possibly she may always be Special Agent Scully. If this is the case, then that in itself is no mean feat, having played the joint lead role in one of television's most successful sci-fi shows of all time, and breaking through many of the sexist traditions of

the industry, simultaneously becoming a role model for many. Maybe in time she will go on to establish herself as one of the world's most accomplished and respected actresses. Maybe, thirty years from now, Gillian will write her own autobiography entitled 'I Am Not Scully'. Who knows?

It's a weird world . . .